My Path of Youth

My Path of Youth

Hiromasa Ikeda

Published by World Tribune Press
606 Wilshire Boulevard
Santa Monica, CA 90401

© 2008 Hiromasa Ikeda
English translation © Soka Gakkai, 2008
All rights reserved.

This book contains essays adapted from a series that originally appeared in *Koko Shimpo* (June 2002–April 2003), the Soka Gakkai's high school division newspaper.

Printed in the United States of America.
Interior photos and back cover photo courtesy of Seikyo Press
© 2008 Hiromasa Ikeda
Interior and cover design by Gopa & Ted2, Inc.

ISBN 978-1-932911-49-7
10 9 8 7 6 5 4 3 2 1

Table of Contents

Preface   ix

I   THE CHERRY BLOSSOMS OF MY YOUTH

1. My Family and the Spring Cherry Blossoms   1
2. An Original Member of the Future Division   7
3. Youth and Reading   13
4. After College   19
5. The Glow of Fireflies   25

II   TRAVELING THE WORLD ON BEHALF OF MY FATHER

6. A Jubilant Bicentennial in New York   33
7. Honors From Argentina, the Land of Silver   39
8. An Art Exhibition in Spain, Land Rich in Culture   45

9.	In Guangzhou, China: My Father's 100th Academic Honor	51
10.	India, the Birthplace of Buddhism	57
11.	Pioneers of Brazil	65
12.	The Opening of Soka University of America in Aliso Viejo, California	71
13.	A Shared Peace: Cultural and Educational Exchange With Mongolia	77

III   Toward the Century of Human Revolution

14.	Hiroshima: Shaping the Spirit of Humanity	85
15.	The Human Power of Peace	91
16.	The Oneness of Mentor and Disciple: Our Founding Spirit	97
17.	Photographs From a Fully Engaged Life	105
18.	Strong Ties With Ever-Victorious Kansai	111
19.	Karuizawa and the Three Founding Presidents	117

IV   The Philosophy of Peace and the Wellspring of Poetic Sentiment

20.	Lending Courage to Friends Through Poetry	125
21.	The Significance of the "Gandhi, King, Ikeda" Exhibition	131
22.	The Legacy of the Pauling Family	137
23.	Thoughts on Mount Fuji As Seen From Space	143

24.	Bold As Mount Fuji	149
25.	The Hakone Long-Distance Relay	155
26.	To My Friends in Taiwan—Winter Always Turns to Spring	159

V   A GREAT BEACON OF PEACE AND EDUCATION

27.	Address at the First Entrance Ceremony of Soka University of America in Aliso Viejo, California	167
28.	Visiting Morehouse College, the Sanctuary of Civil Rights	171
29.	Soka University of America: Crystallizing the People's Sincerity	175
30.	Address at the Second Entrance Ceremony of Soka University of America in Aliso Viejo, California	179
31.	My Memory of Dunhuang, a Treasure of the World	185
32.	On China's Manned Spaceflight	191

Postscript	195
More on Nichiren Buddhism and Its Application to Daily Life	197

Preface

*The Bodhisattvas of the Earth
have emerged!
They have arisen!
They have started to stir, to move!*

*Here, on the American continent,
the winds of a new era
have begun to blow. . . .*

. . . .

*Your voices, resounding to the heavens,
are earnest, devoted and sincere.*

*That bell
is not an evening bell
but the bell of dawn.*

These lines from the poem "Soar—Into the Vast Skies of Freedom! Into the New Century!"[1] my father wrote and dedicated to the members of the SGI-USA in July 2000.

In that poem, he recounts the thoughts of the first Soka Gakkai president, Tsunesaburo Makiguchi, and the second president, Josei Toda, regarding the United States of America, a nation for which both felt a great fondness.

About a hundred years ago, at the outset of the twentieth century, Mr. Makiguchi said that he saw in America a land where civilizations would meet one day and unite.[2] "It was America," Mr. Toda often told my father, "that brought freedom of religion to postwar Japan, opening the way for our peace movement based on Nichiren Buddhism."

"Daisaku!" he would say, "I want to go to the U.S. to repay our debt of gratitude!"[3] My father avows that to carry on the intent of these two mentors, as their direct disciple, he determined to take the first step in his travels for peace in America.

And immediately after his appointment as the third Soka Gakkai president, my father did, in the autumn of 1960, make the United States the first stop on his journey around the world.

America is the country I also visited for the first time outside Japan. That was in 1976, when the SGI-USA held a nationwide convention in New York City. My father had been scheduled to attend, but a sudden urgent matter prevented him from leaving Japan. It was decided that I would represent him at the New York event. Visiting the United States on numerous occasions since then, I have made friends with many SGI-USA members as well as scholars and cultural leaders who, insightful of the nature of our movement, have warmly watched over us and offered their support.

For me, as for my father, America is a special place that inspires deep thought and fresh resolve. And so, when work began in the United States on this English translation of my essay series *My Path of Youth* for publication as a book, I was deeply appreciative.

I began writing these essays in June 2000, and they were serialized in *Koko Shimpo*, the Soka Gakkai's high school division newspaper. In July 2003, in response to readers' requests, the essays, along with two addresses I delivered at Soka University of America, were published as a book in Japanese. During that three-year period, I had written twenty-six essays.

Writing has never been my specialty. In fact, as a rather weak writer, I found producing each manuscript a challenging exercise. Yet I felt I must in some way repay my debt of gratitude to our second Soka Gakkai president, Josei Toda, the person who gave me the name *Hiromasa*.[4] He expressed his expectation that one day I become a person of literary ability. And so I have continued to write.

Moreover, the exercise of writing these essays afforded me a precious opportunity to deepen my insight as to how spiritually challenging and noble are my father's ongoing efforts to encourage people by setting words to paper.

The groups that make up the future division in the Soka Gakkai were formed in the 1960s—the high school division, founded in June 1964, followed by the junior high school and boys and girls (elementary school) divisions, founded in January and September 1965, respectively.

On January 25, 1965, I was a fifth-grade elementary school student. Though I had yet to enter junior high school, I participated in the ceremony establishing the junior high school division, held at the Soka Gakkai community center in Bunkyo

Ward, Tokyo. I consider myself a member of the first class of the future division. And as a senior alumnus of that division, I feel it is my mission to transmit faithfully what I have learned to our younger members.

A favorite saying of mine is, "Once you become aware of your great mission to spread your wings and soar into the future, your abilities will quickly expand." My father spoke these words at the 1st High School Division General Meeting in 1968.

Taking this guidance in life to heart, many of the senior alumni of the high school division—fledglings at the time—have awakened to their missions, grown in potential and taken flight as adult phoenixes. Today, they are active in many fields in Japan and around the world. Some of them I have mentioned in this book.

Since childhood, I have observed my father from many perspectives. At times, I have seen him as the person of highest responsibility in our religious organization, wholly exerting himself to encourage and protect every member while paying no heed to his own exhaustion. At other times, I have witnessed him interacting warmly with Soka students, from Soka Kindergarten through Soka University, in the manner of a kind and loving father. And on other occasions, I have watched him dedicate time as an author and poet to the work of writing.

Common to these roles is his constant, sincere and earnest effort for the sake of each person's happiness, and for the peace and prosperity of the community in which each person lives.

With all this in mind, if I were to distill my thoughts about this book into one statement, I would say that my intention has been to write, for the sake of future generations, about my firsthand observations and impressions of my father.

The SGI's movement for peace, culture and education has

now spread to 192 countries and territories. This is because, in each of these locations around the world, a determined disciple has stood up to pursue the global path of peace and happiness pioneered by the SGI president. They have continued steadily, in the spirit of disciples striving alongside the SGI president, whom they hold as their mentor. I have grown more keenly aware of this fact as time goes by. I am deeply moved with an irrepressible sense of appreciation when I think of the many people around the world—people of diverse religious and cultural backgrounds, and in various fields of endeavor—who express their profound respect and support for the SGI.

"The Law," Nichiren Daishonin writes, "does not spread by itself: because people propagate it, both people and the Law are worthy of respect."[5] No matter how wonderful a system of thought or philosophy, only when there are people who put it into practice, can its value be known. Today, many such people have emerged and are sincerely and courageously putting the SGI's philosophy into practice. This is why it has developed into a broad global movement.

Though I may possess limited ability, my thought each day is how I can best assist and support this process.

Near the end of the poem, "Soar—Into the Vast Skies of Freedom! Into the New Century!" my father writes:

> *For the sake of*
> *these free, young spirits,*
> *I have determined to spend*
> *the culminating years of my life*
> *in this America I love,*
> *together creating infinite memories,*
> *sounding the reverberant trumpet of the dawn.*[6]

If my fellow SGI members in America, whom my father so dearly loves—in particular, the youth, on whom the future depends—can take up *My Path of Youth* and find in it a little food for thought, a bit of spiritual nourishment, then nothing could bring me greater joy.

With deep appreciation, I thank you of the SGI-USA and others who have made the publication of this work possible.

August 24, 2008
Hiromasa Ikeda

Notes

1. Daisaku Ikeda, *Songs for America: Poems by Daisaku Ikeda* (Santa Monica, CA: World Tribune Press, 2000), pp. 9–30.
2. Tsunesaburo Makiguchi, *A Geography of Human Life*, English ed., Dayle M. Bethel, ed. (San Francisco: Caddo Gap Press), p. 293.
3. *Songs for America: Poems by Daisaku Ikeda*, p. 15.
4. The Chinese character for *hiro* of *Hiromasa*, originally meaning broad or expansive, is a component of the Japanese word for *doctor*, and suggests broad knowledge or erudition. The Chinese character *masa* means right or correct.
5. *Gosho zenshu*, p. 856.
6. *Songs for America: Poems by Daisaku Ikeda*, p. 30.

The Cherry Blossoms of My Youth

1

My Family and the Spring Cherry Blossoms

WHEN I was in elementary school, my family lived in a little house in Tokyo's Ota Ward, which had a flowering cherry tree. My father, being fond of cherry blossoms, had planted it as a small tree. It seemed fitting for our neighborhood, Kobayashi-cho, *kobayashi* meaning "little forest." Cherry trees grow relatively fast, and the tree was already quite tall by the time I was in junior high school. Every year around the beginning of April, it would be in full bloom and truly a sight to behold.

One day, my mother, father and I were on the veranda watching the tree's falling cherry blossoms. My father was reciting a well-known verse that suggested the tragic melancholy of wartime: "Some blossoms fall, and some remain… yet even these will fall." He then asked me, "Hiromasa, you don't like cherry blossoms very much, do you?"

"I neither like nor dislike them," I replied. "But since both you and Mom are watching them, I'm just out here to keep you company."

My father turned to my mother and said with a sigh, "This boy has no sense of the poetic."

"Dad," I tried to counter, "you were in elementary school when the textbooks all began with the phrase, 'Blooming, blooming, the cherry trees are blooming.' So maybe that's why you came to like cherry blossoms." Sometimes my father, while in the bathtub, would sing an old military song that went: "A flower, once it blooms, must resign itself to falling." To express my criticism of this, I went so far as to become critical of cherry blossoms themselves.

I remember my father commenting, as we watched the shower of petals fall to the ground: "You know, flowering cherry trees are not unique to Japan. Some say that they originated in the Himalayas, and others, that they came to Japan from the neighboring Cheju Island near the Korean Peninsula."

Hearing this, I nodded. Certainly, I thought, the cherry tree itself was not to blame for the meanings that came to be associated with it. Its flowers suddenly blooming and then falling and scattering just as quickly—it is a magnificent tree with a graceful presence. The vividly colored petals drifting down from its branches paint a beautiful picture, the very image of serenity and peace.

It was people, the state, who turned the cherry blossom into a symbol of militarism. Wartime nationalists had used the flower as a metaphor for young soldiers going off to die in battle, likening them to "young spring blossoms" scattering in the breeze. Pondering this, I felt a bit sorry for the cherry tree. After all, wasn't its original nature rather feminine, functioning to calm the heart and mind? Was the cherry blossom not a symbol of peace, of Japanese serenity?

As the three of us took in the view of falling cherry blossoms at our home in Kobayashi-cho, it occurred to me how truly vital it is to have peace.

My father once told me, "Since you were born in April, you and the cherry blossoms have a special connection." Those words have never left me. From the end of March into April of the year I was born, it seems, the cherry blossoms were particularly resplendent. I was often told that my maternal grandfather, grandmother, mother and father used to walk together along the banks of the nearby Tama River to view the cherry blossoms.

■ ■ ■ ■ ■

On April 28, 1953, my father accompanied Josei Toda, the second president of the Soka Gakkai, to the Head Temple Taiseki-ji[1] to attend a ceremony celebrating the restoration of the Five-Story Pagoda on the temple grounds. That day was also the 700th anniversary of the date in 1253 when Nichiren Daishonin publicly declared the establishment of his teaching. To honor the occasion, a banquet was held with Nissho, the high priest at the time, and President Toda in attendance.

Later, my father received a telegram that read, "Your wife has given birth to a boy." When he shared this with High Priest Nissho and President Toda, they were extremely happy. That night, President Toda composed a poem:

> *A spring moon*
> *Shares my delight*
> *At the birth of your child.*

With a writing brush, Mr. Toda inscribed these words on the folding fan he carried with him. To this day, that fan is one of our family treasures.

When my father asked President Toda to name his new son, President Toda thought a while. Then, lifting his glasses slightly, he wrote "Hiromasa" with a fountain pen on a piece of stationery, and said: "Isn't it a fine name? He could become a man of letters."

With a smile, he handed the paper to my father.

About a month later, President Toda's wife visited our apartment, then in the Sanno area of Tokyo's Ota Ward. She presented us with Mr. Toda's calling card and a gift of a family heirloom. On the card was written the verse:

> *The great Chinese phoenix takes flight*
> *toward ponds and fields,*
> *soaring broadly, truly*
> *for the sake of the people.*[2]

On June 12 that year (1953), my father received a special family Gohonzon. President Toda came to conduct the Gohonzon enshrinement ceremony in our small room. That was my first encounter with President Toda. I was only four months old at the time.

According to the lease agreement, a family with more than one child was not permitted to live in our apartment, and so, with my brother's birth in January 1955, time came for us to move.

Since my father was rarely home, President Toda suggested that we move closer to my mother's parents' house. In June 1955, we moved to a house in Kobayashi-cho, a ten- or fifteen-minute walk from the home of my maternal grandparents, the Shirakis, in the Yaguchi area. Today, I am aware of how small a house it was, but to a child's eye it seemed as splendid as any mansion.

It was our castle. Before long, though, a road-widening project caused us to move from Kobayashi-cho and took us away from our flowering cherry tree.

■ ■ ■ ■ ■

In September 1966, when I was in my first year as a junior high school student at Keio School, we moved to Shinano-machi in Shinjuku Ward, Tokyo, where the Soka Gakkai Headquarters is located. We rented the house from the Headquarters, which maintained it for staff housing. It had been built many decades earlier, and the second floor added later. Whenever a car passed on the sloping street in front, the entire place shook as if an earthquake had struck.

The house had a tiny yard, where two flowering cherry trees firmly stood their ground. They braved cold winters year after year and bloomed magnificently come each April. My father at one point decided to name the trees.

"Let's call this one the Heian Cherry Tree and that one the Genroku Cherry Tree."[3]

"Well, I guess that's OK," my mother said, not fully convinced, but going along anyway with my father's idea.

I remember telling my mother later, in confidence, "If it were me, I would have called them Father Cherry Tree and Mother Cherry Tree."

We once composed a poem together about those cherry trees. As we stood under a shower of blossoms, I said, "A blizzard of flowers," to which my father added, "on my father's shoulders." My mother ended the poem with the line, "on my mother's hair." This short verse, a joint creation of father, mother and son, is etched deeply in my memory. Years later, when I became a teacher at Kansai Soka High School, the cherry trees that grew around campus had not been well cared for, and I remember working with students to mow the grass around the trees. My desire to do so, I think, stemmed from the connection I've had with cherry trees since my youth.

A poet once wrote, "Oh, cherry blossoms that evoke many memories of mine!"[4] Lately, I have felt that I, too, want to lead a life that is rich with memories linked to cherry blossoms.

Published June 14, 2000

Notes

1. The head temple of Nichiren Shoshu, a school of Buddhist clergy with which the Soka Gakkai was once affiliated. In 1991, Nikken, the high priest of that school, attempted to implement a plan to disband the lay organization. See pages 12 and 100, for more information.
2. The great Chinese phoenix is a mythical creature originating in Chinese literature. Its wingspan is said to cover the entire sky and even reach higher into the heavens, where it visits the great "heavenly pond." This poem, in explaining how the name was chosen, uses some wordplay with the Chinese characters that form the name *Hiromasa Ikeda*. *Ikeda* is made up of the characters *ike* (pond) and *da* (field). *Hiromasa* is made up of the characters *hiro* (far and wide) and *masa* (straight and true). Therefore, the poet seems to be implying that this child will fly far and wide, high into the heavens like the great mythical bird, on behalf of the common people.
3. The Heian Cherry Tree is named after the Heian period of Japanese history (794–1185); *heian* literally means peace and tranquillity. The Genroku Cherry Tree is named after the Genroku era (1688–1704), known as the Golden Age of Japan's Edo period (1603–1868).
4. Matsuo Basho, (1644–94).

2

An Original Member of the Future Division

I CONSIDER MYSELF a member of the "first class" of the Soka Gakkai's future division—collectively comprising the elementary, junior high and high school divisions. This is because I attended the inaugural meeting of the Soka Gakkai junior high school division, held at the Bunkyo Ward Fourth Headquarters (today, the Bunkyo Hall of Peace), in Tokyo, on January 15, 1965. I was only in the fifth grade, but the junior high school division then included fifth- and sixth-grade students. To attend the meeting, I traveled all the way to Bunkyo Ward, centrally located among Tokyo's twenty-three wards, from Ota Ward, in the extreme south.

At the time there were two systems of organization in the Soka Gakkai, the horizontal system and vertical system. The horizontal system was similar to the one we have today, designed geographically, with members gathering as districts in their local neighborhoods. The vertical system grouped members according to personal connections; that is, new members joined the same district that the person who introduced them to the Soka

Gakkai belonged to, regardless of geographical location. (Our Soka Gakkai of today was built on the vertical system; as the membership grew, the horizontal, or geographical, system became the standard.)

My father had been assigned, under the vertical system, as acting leader to Bunkyo Chapter in 1952; because of that connection, I was invited to attend the junior high school division inaugural ceremony in Bunkyo Ward. It was at this event that the youth division leader of the time presented us students with five guidelines:

1. Let's keep up a consistent practice of gongyo.
2. Let's study hard.
3. Let's have good attendance at school.
4. Let's not cause our parents to worry.
5. Let's live each day honestly, strongly and cheerfully.

It seems that my father had given these guidelines the previous day to the youth division leader, though I didn't know this at the time. Had I heard these same points directly from my own parent, I probably would not have taken them to heart. But hearing them from one of our leaders at this Soka Gakkai meeting, I resolved to put them into practice. It was then, for the first time, as a second-generation Soka Gakkai member born into the Buddhist practice, that I really felt like a full-fledged member in my own right. It was also the first time I determined to fulfill specific goals through my Buddhist practice.

After my two younger brothers became members of the future division, I would bring them with me to Bunkyo Ward for activities. Sometimes we did not want to go, because the activity was so far away. I remember my mother telling us on those occasions: "You may look forward to going out and playing, but coming home afterward, all you feel is tired. When you attend a Soka Gakkai activity, even if you don't feel like going, you come home refreshed." We grew to see that she was right.

Although I referred to myself as a second-generation Soka Gakkai member, I am in fact a third-generation member on my mother's side. My maternal grandparents began to practice Nichiren Buddhism in 1941, when my mother was nine years old. They were devoted to faith since the early days of the Soka Gakkai, practicing alongside presidents Makiguchi and Toda.

My grandparents were very fond of me, and as a child I spent a good portion of my time at their home. Because their home had long been a venue for discussion meetings, from an early age I naturally felt part of the Soka Gakkai family.

My grandfather died in 1981. My grandmother was with us until 2000. She became ill in May that year but recovered somewhat in July, in time to celebrate the sixtieth anniversary of her conversion to Nichiren Buddhism. Then, on August 24, she died at age ninety-five, having lived a wonderful, meaningful life.

■ ■ ■ ■ ■

On June 7, 1964, the high school division was established. The following year saw the formation of both the junior high school division (in January) and the elementary school division (in September). The future division as we know it today was thus complete.

On January 3, 1966, representatives of the inaugural class of each division (high school, junior high school and elementary school) from throughout Japan gathered at the head temple, Taiseki-ji.[1] I, a sixth-grader, and my brother Shirohisa, a fifth-grader, attended as junior high school division members. My youngest brother, Takahiro, then in the first grade, attended the gathering as a member of the elementary school division. Most of the participants were high school students and took care of us as if they were our older brothers.

When we posed for a commemorative photo together in front of the Grand Reception Hall,[2] those of us in elementary school were seated in the front row. I still have this photo as a memento of that day. We also planted a Himalayan cedar, and whenever I went to the head temple, I always looked forward to seeing how tall the tree had grown.

At the January 3, 1966, event—a national meeting for the high school division at the Grand Reception Hall—my father said, "I propose that all of us here today meet again five years hence, on January 3, 1971." Sure enough, five years later, in January 1971, we held another gathering, and the participants became known as the Five-Year Group. From that time on, we met every five years, and all three of us brothers attended these meetings together.

In time, the Himalayan cedar we had planted was gone, and the Grand Reception Hall, sadly, was destroyed by Nikken[3] out of malice and jealousy. But he could never destroy the memories we formed and determinations we made during those days.

In January 1966, my father started a monthly series of lectures for the high school division. I had just entered junior high school that April, but was allowed to attend these lectures. This was when I began to study Nichiren Daishonin's writings in earnest. Among the writings we studied was "Letter from Sado," which is still one of my favorites. The members who attended these lectures were named the Young Phoenix Group. Although I was still young for the group, they included me as a member.

On August 15, 1969, while in my first year of high school, I attended the 2nd High School Division General Meeting at the Nihon University Auditorium. Summer training for my high school track and field team had ended just the day before, and I would have much preferred to stay home and rest. But one of the high school division leaders encouraged me to go with him, and I reluctantly tagged along. Thinking back on it, I am very grateful to him for giving me the opportunity to attend. At the meeting, my father proposed: "Let us all meet again thirty years from today, in the year 2000!" From then on, we were known as the Year 2000 Group and looked forward to meeting again in 2000, which seemed so far off in the future.

This month (September 2000), the commemorative meeting of the Year 2000 Group was held jointly with the future division general meeting at the Soka University Auditorium, in Hachioji, Tokyo. Current members of the future division gathered with the original members from thirty years before! This time, the young future division attendees were encouraged to "look thirty years ahead, to the year 2030, when we will commemorate the one-hundredth anniversary of the Soka Gakkai's founding."

At the meeting, the SGI president was awarded the Mahatma M. K. Gandhi Millennium Award for Non-violent Peace, making it a most fitting gathering for the year 2000.

For all the future division alumni involved, attending this historic event resulted directly from having attended the 1969 high school division general meeting. I feel that now is the time for me to make a powerful resolution that will serve as my personal cause toward celebrating, thirty years from now, the brilliant centennial of the Soka Gakkai's founding.

Published September 27, 2000

Notes

1. Taiseki-ji—The head temple of the Nichiren Shoshu priesthood.
2. Grand Reception Hall—A structure built and donated to the head temple Taiseki-ji by the Soka Gakkai.
3. Nikken—The sixty-seventh high priest of Nichiren Shoshu from 1979 to 2005, who developed a strong animosity toward the Soka Gakkai and SGI President Ikeda, and embarked on an unsuccessful course of trying to destroy the organization of the Soka Gakkai International. He demolished buildings on the Taiseki-ji grounds that had been donated by the Soka Gakkai—including the Grand Reception Hall and the Sho-Hondo, or Grand Main Temple, built in 1972 through the sincere donations of Soka Gakkai members.

3

Youth and Reading

THERE IS an old book in my bookcase—*Napoleon* by Yusuke Tsurumi, published in 1931—that belonged to my father. He may have bought it at a secondhand bookstore in Kanda, or perhaps gotten it through a book club he and some neighborhood friends started when they were teenagers. On the first blank page appear the words my father had written as a young man, "To my dear Hiromasa, from Daisaku." I suppose he had hopes that I would read it someday. The book, however, is written in old kana orthography, which uses difficult-to-read Chinese characters to spell Western names such as *Napoleon* and *France*. I did not feel up to the challenge of reading it until my first year in high school, when the book was published in a modern, more readable, paperback edition.

I am not entirely certain when I developed the habit of reading books, but do remember my father's vast book collection in the family bookcase. Accustomed to seeing the writing on the spines of those books as I grew up, I naturally came to remember their titles and authors. Yet I hesitated to take any of them from the shelf, as they were either handsomely boxed or looked very old and valuable.

When I was in elementary school, my two brothers and I would regularly make the trip from Ota Ward, where we lived, to the Soka Gakkai Headquarters in Shinano-machi. After we visited with our father there, he would often bring us to a nearby bookstore where he would buy us books after telling us each to pick out any three we wanted. Thanks to this routine, I grew accustomed to choosing books on my own.

It was in high school that I began to make a conscious effort to read widely. On the first page of my reading notebook from those days, I see that I listed the following under the heading "Principles for Reading":

1. Deeply grasp the author's intent.
2. Thoroughly read and comprehend the content of each book.
3. Absorb even more deeply the parts that you like.
4. Read first-rate newspapers and magazines.

I had copied these points from *The Twenty-first Century Pioneer*, a pamphlet containing a collection of educational guidelines for the Soka Gakkai high school division.

"Great Books" is a reading program that began in the United States. As I understand it, books on its reading list are those that have been read by a great many people over the centuries and are still relevant today, books that one can benefit from rereading and books that are instructive to many. To read extraordinary works that meet such criteria, I feel, can lead to profound enrichment in life.

The time of youth, I think, is an opportunity to seek and encounter such great works.

While in high school, I made it my goal to read one book per week, four books per month and fifty books per year. *The Twenty-first Century Pioneer* listed one hundred books as suggested reading, and I recall challenging myself to read as many as I could. To look over the titles listed in my reading notebook vividly brings back the emotions I felt when I read some of those works. There are also some whose content I don't remember at all. Nevertheless, taking on the challenge of reading those books remains a fond memory.

If I were to categorize the books listed in my reading notebook, they would be roughly as follows:

Classic Japanese literary works, including: *I Am a Cat* by Soseki Natsume, *Rashomon* by Ryunosuke Akutagawa, *The Setting Sun* by Osamu Dazai, *The Beautiful Village* by Tatsuo Hori, *Ango kodan* by Ango Sakaguchi, *Friendship* by Mushanokoji Saneatsu, *Night of the Milky Way Railway* by Kenji Miyazawa, *Hikawa seiwa* by Katsu Kaishu and *Collection of Essays* by Torahiko Terada.

World literary works, including: *The Count of Monte Cristo* by Alexandre Dumas, *Ninety-Three* by Victor Hugo, *Taras Bulba* by Nikolai Gogol, *Joseph Fouché* by Stefan Zweig and *The Best Short Stories of O. Henry* by O. Henry.

Literary works by popular Japanese writers, including: *Snow Country* by Yasunari Kawabata, *The Sound of Waves* by Yukio Mishima, *The Roof Tile of Tempyo* by Yasushi Inoue, *Date Masamune* by Sohachi Yamaoka, *Yoshitsune* by Ryotaro Shiba, *Kaze ni soyogu ashi* (Reeds Waving in the Breeze) by Tatsuzo Ishikawa, *Rakujitsu moyu* (Burning Sunset) by Saburo Shiroyama, *Inspector Imanishi Investigates* (*Suna no utsuwa*) by Seicho Matsumoto and *Seishun no mon* (The Gate of Youth) by Hiroyuki Itsuki.

In 1968, the Japanese novelist Yasunari Kawabata won the

Nobel Prize in Literature. I was in my third year of junior high school, and the news motivated me to read some of his works.

I began reading works by Ryotaro Shiba when my father gave me a copy of *Kaido wo yuku* (Travels by the Old Highways). On the very last page, my father had written, "Finished reading on March 20, 1969." Judging from this, I must have read it right after entering high school. I then read in succession four books by Shiba on Japan's Warring States Period: *Kunitori monogatari* (Tale of the Nation Thieves), *Shinshi taikoki* (The New Historical Record of the Taiko), *Sekigahara* (named for the site of an epic battle in 1600) and *Josai* (Fortress). From these readings, I realized for the first time that books about history could be inspiring.

I think that my encounter with some books back then also influenced my becoming a teacher of Japanese history. These include *Maboroshi no yamataikoku* (The Illusory Country of Yamatai) by Kohei Miyazaki, *Iwajuku no hatten* (The Discovery of the Archaeological Site at Iwajuku) by Tadahiro Aizawa and *Showashi hakkutsu* (Excavations in Showa History) by Seicho Matsumoto.

■ ■ ■ ■ ■

In the 1931 edition of Yusuke Tsurumi's *Napoleon*, there is a picture of the house in Corsica where Napoleon was born. I never imagined I would actually go there, but in July 1998, an opportunity arose for me to visit the island. We had received word that the mayor of Corsica, who had read and been moved by my father's writings, including his peace proposals, wished to present my father with a medal of recognition. I went to Corsica to accept the award on my father's behalf.

Now a territory of France, the island of Corsica has suffered a long and bitter history of oppression by one foreign occupier after another, due to its strategic location in the Mediterranean. Because of this, all the more does the desire for peace run strong there. The mayor told me that, perhaps more than anyone anywhere in the world, the people of Corsica wish to see the fruition of the SGI's philosophy of peace in their homeland. Before this encounter, my image of Corsica had been that of a small island. To my surprise, however, it is half the size of Shikoku (one of the four main islands of Japan) and, at its heights, reaches nearly nine thousand feet. The undulating terrain gives the impression of a mountain towering over the sea.

The house where Napoleon was born is a four-story building on a narrow lane in a bustling section of the town of Ajaccio. An unassuming structure, it would go unnoticed were it not for the many tourists around it. In his book *The Social Contract and Discourses*, French philosopher Jean-Jacques Rousseau presciently observes, "I have a feeling that some day that little island will astonish Europe."[1] Perhaps in line with Rousseau's prediction, Corsica did produce an epoch-making hero in the person of Napoleon.

In his book *A Geography of Human Life*, Tsunesaburo Makiguchi theorizes that islands, being open to broad cultural influences by virtue of their location along sea routes, can be the birthplaces of new culture.[2]

Following the award ceremony at which the medal was presented, I posed for pictures with members of the Corsica Chapter of SGI-France at a nearby beach. My heartfelt prayer was that heroes of the Mystic Law, who look toward the coming age with fresh energy and vitality, will continue to emerge and develop on this island.

Each time I pick up the book *Napoleon*, I wonder what my father's thoughts and determinations were when he read it as a youth. On another blank page of the book is a line he wrote back then in his vibrant, youthful hand: "Each time a wave encounters an obstacle, its strength increases."

Published October 25, 2000

NOTES:

1. Jean-Jacques Rousseau, *The Social Contract and Discourses*, trans. G. D. H. Cole (London: J.M. Dent and Sons, Limited, 1950), p. 224.
2. *A Geography of Human Life*—Written by Tsunesaburo Makiguchi, the revolutionary Japanese educator who founded the Soka Gakkai (Value-Creating Society) and became its first president. He devoted much consideration to the relationship between life and education, developing his theories on the creation of value, the happiness of the individual and the prosperity of society at large. Typical of his work is his first book, *Jinsei chirigaku* (A Geography of Human Life), published in 1903. See Tsunesaburo Makiguchi, *A Geography of Human Life*, English ed., Dayle M. Bethel, ed. (San Francisco: Caddo Gap Press, 1903), p. 293.

4

After College

JUST BEFORE graduating college, I was talking one day with several schoolmates at a coffee shop near our campus, when the conversation turned to finding employment. The exchange was bright and cheerful: One friend reported being hired by a well-known corporation; another, by a major manufacturer; and another, by a famous department store.

As for me, I had yet to make up my mind about what I would do next. I had considered the possibilities of studying abroad and becoming a scholar but hadn't settled on anything specific. From then on, though, I prayed more earnestly than ever to the Gohonzon for clarity. Years later, I learned that representatives of several leading firms had directly approached my father to offer me jobs. He never mentioned this to me, however.

It was sometime near the end of my elementary school days, as I recall, that a foreign journalist came to interview my family. At some point in the conversation, my brothers and I were asked, "What kind of person would you like to become when you grow up?" In unison, we replied, "Someone like Daddy!" The interviewer laughed and jokingly said, "Having three Soka

Gakkai presidents could be a problem." At our age, of course, we had no idea what sort of position the president of the Soka Gakkai was, nor did we understand what kind of activities our father was engaged in. We simply knew that we wanted to become like him.

"There is no need for you to become great or famous people," our father would tell us from time to time, even when we were older. "Actually, I'd prefer that you not. All I care about is that you remain true to the correct path of faith and do your best for the sake of the Soka Gakkai, whatever your position in life. Working devotedly within the Soka Gakkai is directly connected to world peace and every other aspect of life."

While I was still pondering my career path, my mother commented once after our evening prayers: "Recognizing and repaying debts of gratitude are among the highest human virtues. You owe a great deal to the Soka Gakkai, so please do something to show your appreciation." With those words, I decided what I had to do.

There was an opening for a social studies teacher at Kansai Soka High School, and I was fortunate enough to be offered the job. My mother supported my decision to accept and said to me: "You were born and raised in Tokyo; instead of staying here, it will be good for you to work hard and experience life away from home. This will be an asset to you in the future." And so I was off to Osaka, the place where my father had created unforgettable memories in his youth.[1]

■ ■ ■ ■ ■

The Soka Gakkai began as a group of educators known as the Soka Kyoiku Gakkai, the Value-Creating Education Society.

While it has evolved into an organization devoted to the spread of Buddhism, a noted scholar has praised our organization as a "university of humanism." Indeed, there seems to be no other religious group that encourages not only the study of Buddhism, but also the reading of literary prose and poetry and the singing of songs, utilizing creative ways of learning to introduce and convey the ideals of Buddhism.

When I first awoke to faith in Buddhism, I remember being deeply impressed with President Toda's statement that reason enhances faith, and faith, in turn, seeks reason. It meant to me that our faith is consistent with sound reason, that the Buddhism we embrace accords with the principles of society.

Both first and second presidents Makiguchi and Toda were educators, and my father, their successor, has poured a tremendous amount of effort and energy into education. He once told me, "President Makiguchi said that, although one function of education is to gain knowledge, its ultimate purpose is to create a happy person." I have always felt that there is something amiss in a society that overly emphasizes academic credentials and gives little attention to the development of the whole person.

Having these things in mind, naturally I wrestled with the fundamental questions of why, what and how an educator should go about teaching students. Many teachers, of course, simply went forth to teach without giving these concerns much thought. Such was the state of education at the time. The fact that I was able to develop a personal sense of mission as a teacher is something I attribute to those words of Mr. Makiguchi passed along to me by my father. And so I was determined that Kansai Soka Schools would become an institution that fully actualizes Mr. Makiguchi's thoughts, spirit and objectives for education.

My father told me when I was hired to teach: "Please take

care of your health and do your absolute best for the schools and each of your students. Setting yourself a goal of ten years, give your all to the endeavor with patience and perseverance. That's the way to ensure victory for yourself, your students and the schools."

And my mother said to me: "If this were a time of war, every man would have to join the military and be sent to the battlefront. If you look at it from that perspective, there's no better time to live than right now, a time of peace. Don't forget how fortunate you are."

■ ■ ■ ■ ■

In April 1978, on my first day as a teacher at Kansai Soka High School, I was full of energy and enthusiasm. The students, too, were full of life, and the campus also seemed vibrant and alive. I was brimming with appreciation and joy for the opportunity to foster each of these eager and pure-hearted students, these leaders of the twenty-first century, whose eyes glowed with excitement for the future. As I stood in class and addressed my students for the first time, I declared in my heart that I would provide them with an education that would enable every one of them to find happiness.

While I was teaching at Kansai Soka High School, my younger brother Shirohisa completed graduate school at Soka University and joined the faculty there. And my youngest brother, Takahiro, graduated from Soka University and became a teacher at Kansai Soka Elementary School. I remember our father telling us at that time, "The three of you together represent a complete and well-rounded Soka education." My mother also seemed pleased.

"Education is neither a right nor an obligation. It is a most important mission." This was the maxim our father, the founder of Soka Schools, gave to us as educators.

■ ■ ■ ■ ■

The ten years toward which my father had advised me to aim in my teaching career came to an end in 1988. That year, I left my teaching post and joined the staff of the Soka Gakkai Headquarters. Those ten years seemed to pass in the blink of an eye, yet they are ten golden years I shall never forget.

I am very happy to report that faculty members, both senior and junior to me, with whom I shared sweat and tears working to develop the school, now form the core of Soka education. Also, there is no greater source of pride and joy for a teacher than to witness the growth of one's students. That is truly a delight unique to those in the teaching profession. And now, as I see my former students active in many fields and disciplines, in their communities as well as in the Soka Schools, I am confident that a mighty tradition of Soka education has been established.

Published August 9, 2000

NOTE

1. In 1956, second Soka Gakkai president Josei Toda sent his young disciple, Daisaku Ikeda, to Osaka.

5

The Glow of Fireflies

"The glow of the firefly, the snow on the windowpane…"[1] This song, "Glow of the Fireflies," is traditionally sung at school graduation ceremonies throughout Japan, and singing it along with my fellow students remains an unforgettable memory of my own graduation.

I began teaching social studies at Kansai Soka High School in April 1978 and remember marveling at the school's wondrous setting and its scenes of campus life: The school building, Man'yo Pond, the Katano Mountains, determined students walking briskly up the paths leading to campus—everything signaled new growth. There were poetry and song, perseverance and hope. Everything was wonderful!

The seemingly timeless city of Katano is nestled dreamlike amid an ideal setting of lush greenery, rivers and mountains. There is the small, elegantly named Genji Falls. The Hotaru ("Firefly") River, running alongside the school grounds, took its name from the way it beautifully reflected the light of fireflies above it. And the nearby Amano River is named after the Milky Way, which is said to reflect perfectly on its surface.[2]

Having moved from the hustle and bustle of Tokyo, I now found myself amid this wonderful natural environment, a completely new experience. It was to me a palace for the heart, a noble refuge of learning and intellect.

Springtime graced the landscape with lovely flowers. The summers were pleasant, and I recall there being a vineyard nearby. The parade of abundant greenery and blossoms composed a timeless portrait, one that could drive away any hint of sadness.

A little brook running through our school with fireflies dancing overhead evoked a classic scene from Japan's Heian period. I wanted my parents to see this; indeed, I wanted many people to see it.

■ ■ ■ ■ ■

Soon after I joined the faculty, we had a meeting with the school founder, my father. As we talked about the school's lush natural surroundings, he suggested: "Why don't we call the fireflies back to this land of the Hotaru River? Their disappearance is most likely due to increasing environmental pollution."[3] And, he added, "Why not plant flowering cherry trees so that they will be in full bloom to welcome the new students in the spring?" Though a bit surprised by his sudden proposals, we all expressed our agreement.

"As to who will be in charge of these projects, I'll leave that to you to decide among yourselves." Our founder's clear and resolute voice inspired resolve in each of us.

Fresh hope emerged among us and with it a renewed sense of mission to build a new stronghold of wisdom and intellect.

We quickly called for a faculty meeting to discuss the projects. Mr. Shigeo Matsuo, a math teacher, volunteered to head the firefly project. By consensus, Mr. Miyata, a music teacher at Kansai Soka Elementary School, was asked to head the cherry tree project. Both teachers had the deep trust and respect of the founder; they were earnest and resolute, and passionate in their mission of Soka education.

In the early morning chill before classes began, Mr. Matsuo would go to a nearby rice field and collect the marsh snails that fireflies feed on. These were essential to a thriving firefly population. Farmers in their fields eyed him quizzically, unsure of what he might be up to. At some point, it seems, he was even questioned by police. But none of that deterred him from his morning routine.

Someone once shouted at him: "Hey, what are you doing down there? You're not going to find any money in that ditch!"

Still, diligently and steadily, he kept at it, gathering snails and laying the groundwork for the fireflies to take flight. It was a tough job, and few acknowledged his hard work; some of his colleagues even mocked him. But through it all, Mr. Matsuo remained committed to bringing the glow of fireflies to our campus and fulfilling the founder's vision.

By the end of May the following year (1979), fireflies at last began dancing above our little brook!

A full seven years later, on June 20, 1986, in the quiet of early evening just before sunset, so as not to disturb anyone else, four of us—my father and mother, Mr. Matsuo and I—went off together to watch the fireflies. The scene we witnessed was dreamlike: hundreds of them dancing through the air, crisscrossing paths in an unforgettable and breathtaking performance. "It's as if we've been transported back to the Heian era," my father commented. "I want to name them the Heian Fireflies—

truly, a sight to behold!" It seemed to me he had rarely been as awestruck as at that moment.

Lines from a childhood song came to mind:

Come, fireflies!
That water is bitter,
This water is sweet!
Come, fireflies!

Free to illuminate the skies with the glow that is their mission, they expend themselves fully, bathing their brief existence in brilliance. Their stately dance moved us deeply. Even now, when that time of year comes around, my parents reminisce about the scene they witnessed that evening.

■ ■ ■ ■ ■

I cannot forget my father once sternly cautioning a group of Soka Schools teachers: "These students are the leaders of the future, which means they are more precious to me than if they were my own children. In fact, I cherish them even more so, as my true children. Take care not to scold them indiscriminately. In other words, I want you to nurture them with the greatest consideration and care."

By the same token, my father on many occasions reminded me of the great asset Mr. Matsuo had been to the faculty at Kansai Soka High School, and that Mr. Miyata had likewise contributed greatly as a teacher at Kansai Soka Elementary School. Always treat them with the utmost respect and care, my father would say, just as my mother would remind me to listen carefully to their ideas and advice.

The populations of fireflies that emerged from our school

have continued to expand their range of light to include Soka University and all of Japan. This is due to the efforts of people who have taken to heart the founder's words and put them into action. The heart of Soka education, I feel, resides in this spirit.

Later that evening, after observing the fireflies, my father composed the following three verses:

> *The ancient age of Heian*
> *seems to sparkle*
> *in this firefly light.*
>
> *Graceful jewels*
> *flickering through the skies*
> *over Firefly Pond.*
>
> *Genji fireflies*
> *shimmering in the trees*
> *hark back to the Heian dynasty.*

Published June 28, 2000

Notes

1. This is the first line of a song traditionally sung at Japanese school graduations, to the tune of "Auld Lang Syne."
2. In Japanese, a name for the Milky Way is Amanogawa, literally "the celestial river"; the name of the Amano River mentioned here is also pronounced "Amanogawa" in Japanese. *Ama* means "heaven," and *gawa* (a phonetic variant of *kawa*) means "river."
3. In order to bring clarity to the English translation, a line is added from the SGI Newsletter published version of this event. See the SGI Newsletter 6483, dated June 7, 2005.

Traveling the World
on Behalf of My Father

6

A Jubilant Bicentennial in New York

On July 4, 1976, the bicentennial of the founding of the United States of America, Soka Gakkai International-USA (then known as NSA) held its annual general meeting. My father had planned to attend, but unforeseen circumstances prevented him from leaving Japan. At age twenty-three, I was designated to attend as his representative, accompanying Soka Gakkai Vice President Satoru Izumi.

One evening before our departure, I had finished reciting the sutra with my parents at home when my mother said to me: "Mr. Izumi is a treasured pillar of the Soka Gakkai, a great contributor to our movement since President Makiguchi's time. Accompanying him on this trip will surely become a fond memory for you."

"Mr. Izumi is a wonderful person of excellent character," my father added. "But since he spent the war as a soldier in Southeast Asia, I wonder if he can speak any English."

My mother chuckled and said, "Yes, his Chinese might be better than his English!"

Again, my mother reminded me, "You must always value and respect pioneers like Mr. Izumi who have been of distinguished service to the Soka Gakkai since its very beginning."

That year, after graduating from the Faculty of Law of my university, I entered the Faculty of Letters to obtain my teacher's certificate. On July 1, after my afternoon class, I hurried to Tokyo's Haneda International Airport. The flight to New York took nearly twenty hours, with stopovers in Anchorage and Chicago. As I remember it, though, the hours seemed to pass in the blink of an eye. It was my first trip on my father's behalf, and to a city completely unknown to me. My sense of responsibility, mixed with curiosity and apprehension, made me forget about the passage of time.

Bright sunlight bathed New York on my visit that July. The heat of the surging crowds matched the sweltering temperatures. From the observation deck on the 107th floor of the World Trade Center, I looked out over one of the world's greatest cities. People of diverse backgrounds thrived in this cosmopolitan city, coming and going, shaking hands, doing business, working, studying. It seemed to me a microcosm of an ideal world. I was therefore impressed by the foresight that had led to the choice of New York as the site of the United Nations Headquarters.

■ ■ ■ ■ ■

Incidentally, on June 12, 2000, my father received an honorary doctorate from the Sri Sri Sitaramdas Omkarnath Institute of Sanskrit Learning. Among the school officials attending that ceremony in Japan was Gopal Mitra, a vice chancellor of the Academy and one of the designers of the World Trade Center.

A week later (on June 20), news reached Japan of a subway

train derailment in New York, in which dozens of people were injured. My father quickly contacted SGI leaders in New York to make sure our members were safe. Thankfully, none had been hurt. Observing my father's immediate concern for the members upon hearing of an incident even so far away has always served as a lesson for me. It demonstrates the sense of responsibility that comes with being a leader in our movement to spread the ideals of Buddhism worldwide.

■ ■ ■ ■ ■

On the eve of the general meeting, the members put on a parade in the streets of Manhattan. This grand and lively spectacle, with performers clad in splendid costumes, one might have mistaken for a dream. Thirty-six hundred SGI members assembled from every state in the union, Puerto Rico and Mexico to march. Brass bands, fife and drum corps, dancers and ornate parade floats depicted episodes from two hundred years of American history, beginning with the American Revolution. All along the route, which stretched for well over a mile, a diverse and enthusiastic crowd of citizens cheered on the parade. A sense of peace and joy prevailed as people of many nationalities and ethnicities joined in solidarity. A powerful sense of friendship flowed through them like a wave cresting in each person's heart.

Appearances by celebrities and notables such as Elizabeth Taylor and Governor George Ariyoshi of Hawaii, along with a spectacular fireworks display in Central Park, marked the finale of the evening's festivities. The surge of delight became shouts of joy that arose from the crowd.

The next day, July 4, some ten thousand SGI members made their way proudly to the general meeting site, the Louis

Armstrong Memorial Stadium, in the New York borough of Queens. Attendees, dressed in period costumes reminiscent of the days of the Declaration of Independence, cheered in response to messages from several prominent figures including US President Gerald Ford and Vice President Nelson Rockefeller. My father also sent a message, which I delivered. I fondly recall staying up late into the night before the meeting to work on my delivery in English, an American youth division member coaching me on my pronunciation so that the members could understand me.

On stage, amid roaring applause, a presentation was made of a replica of the Liberty Bell, which I received on behalf of the Soka Gakkai. That bell, which we now call the Twenty-first Century Bell, stands today in front of the main auditorium of Soka University in Tokyo. Its toll can be heard throughout the campus, welcoming all who visit the university from around the world. The faces of members from around the United States shone with radiance, sincerity, cheerfulness and great pride in their faith. America felt to me like a truly free country, one that respected and valued liberty. This freedom included responsibility, natural for a nation of such remarkable achievements.

My father, unable to attend the general meeting in New York, paid a visit to the official residence of the US Ambassador to Japan in Tokyo on July 3 to offer his congratulations on the bicentennial of American independence. On that visit, he asked the ambassador to deliver a personal letter he had written to US President Ford. The next day, he went to the Fuji Art Museum in Shizuoka to view an exhibition of Soviet and Russian national treasures.

This brings to mind the sentiment of Russian literary master Anton Chekhov when he wrote that conceit and arrogance are vices that have no place in the refined heart. I remember Mr. Izumi on this trip being very stern in cautioning the Japanese-born top leaders of the American SGI organization, "Never be arrogant!" Certainly faith means to serve the members, no matter the leaders' position or culture, with heartfelt sincerity; doing so provides the necessary impetus for peace based on Buddhist ideals.

It might be interesting to note that the current SGI-USA general director, Danny Nagashima, and the Soka University of America president, Daniel Habuki, were at that time university students in the United States. Both served as volunteer support staff for this meeting.

■ ■ ■ ■ ■

Twenty years later, in May 1996, I had the opportunity to visit New York again. Though only a stopover of a few hours on my way to South America, it afforded me time to visit the newly opened SGI-USA New York Culture Center. The structure, built more than one hundred years earlier, has a long and distinguished history. Its conversion into an SGI culture center signaled its revival as a cultural edifice and was well received in the local community.

The following month (June 1996), my father made his first visit in fifteen years to New York, to deliver a lecture at Columbia University's Teachers College. At the New York Culture Center, he met with New York members, for whom he composed the following *waka* poem:

New York,
serene and at last triumphant,

*you have created a record
invincible and immortal.*[1]

My first visit to New York—my first trip on my father's behalf—remains for me an enduring memory, an unforgettable page from the record of my youth. Today it is very gratifying to see that the New York SGI has developed into such a robust organization.

The year 2001 marks the 225th anniversary of American Independence. It is also the year by which my father had resolved to open, as his final project, Soka University of America. I wonder what kind of people will be venturing out into the world from SUA on the 250th anniversary of American Independence. I have made a solemn vow to live long enough to see those valiant figures with my own eyes.

Published July 12, 2000

Note

1. Daisaku Ikeda, *My Dear Friends in America* (Santa Monica, CA: World Tribune Press, 2001), p. 443.

7

Honors From Argentina, the Land of Silver

It happened one morning in 1990, at SGI-USA's Malibu Training Center on the outskirts of Los Angeles, situated atop a bluff overlooking the Pacific Ocean. My parents and I had enjoyed a refreshing recitation of the sutra together, when my father said he had a favor to ask of me. Sunlight flooded the room as my mother gazed calmly at both of us in her usual manner. My father, speaking with great care, said: "As it turns out, I can't continue on to South America as planned, so I'd like you to go in my place. Of particular concern is the invitation I received from the president of Argentina, so I would like you to convey to him my deepest apologies for being unable to meet with him."

■ ■ ■ ■ ■

In 1960, six months after becoming the third president of the Soka Gakkai, my father had traveled to the United States, Brazil and other countries, where the number of Soka Gakkai members was still very few. In doing so, he solidified the foundation for the worldwide spread of Nichiren Buddhism. The year 1990 marked the thirtieth anniversary of that voyage. To kick off a new chapter in our global movement, and with an eye toward the twenty-first century, he planned to travel to the United States, Brazil, Argentina and Paraguay. The trip was to last about one month, from February to March.

During the United States portion of the journey, which began with the 11th SGI General Meeting, my father attended successive study sessions with each of the four-divisional groups (the women's, men's, young women's and young men's divisions), pouring his entire heart and soul into encouraging the participants. He also held dialogues with well-known American icons such as Linus Pauling, the father of modern chemistry; Norman Cousins, the journalist and anti-nuclear activist who also advocated care of the human spirit as essential to health; and Armand Hammer, an industrialist and art collector, also influential as an unofficial diplomat. These encounters resulted in lively exchanges of opinion on wide-ranging topics critical to the future course of humanity.

The intensity of his schedule took its toll. Considering the stern advice of his physician and others accompanying him on the trip, he was left with no choice but to cancel his visit to South America. Each country on his itinerary, however, had gone to considerable lengths to welcome him. It was to be, in particular, my father's first visit to Argentina, where the country's president had planned to meet with him and present him with the national medal of honor. In view of this, Mr. Kazuo Oshida, then general director of the SGI-Argentina, strongly urged that my father send me as his representative. To maintain good faith with the country's leaders and to honor the SGI members' wishes, it was agreed that I make what would turn out to be not only my first visit to South America, but my first experience representing my father at a state function.

On February 20, I left the Malibu Training Center for the eleven-hour flight from Los Angeles to Brazil. Once there, immersed in South America's mid-summer heat—a sharp contrast to the February weather in Japan—I attended events that included the São Paulo Art Museum opening of the Treasures of Japanese Art exhibition, on loan from the Tokyo Fuji Art Museum, and the opening of the SGI-Brazil Nature and Culture Center. I then boarded a plane for Argentina.

■ ■ ■ ■ ■

More than four hundred years ago, Europeans came to Argentina in search of silver and other treasures. Today the majority of the population is of European descent, and the capital city of Buenos Aires, where shops and houses neatly line its streets, is called the Paris of South America.

On March 1, the University of Buenos Aires bestowed an honorary doctorate on my father in a ceremony held at the school's auditorium. Among those in attendance was university rector Dr. Oscar Shuberoff. A national school with more than two hundred thousand students, the University of Buenos Aires was founded in 1821 and is Argentina's leading institution of higher learning. On my father's behalf, I delivered the acceptance speech he had prepared.

Even in my student days, I had sensed the increasing influence of Spanish as a world language and, for a time, took Spanish lessons at a language school. People say that Spanish is easy for Japanese people to pronounce, but I ended my studies without becoming very good at it. On that day at the University of Buenos Aires, I regretted having to deliver the speech in Japanese, thinking that I could have done it in Spanish had I studied harder.

The next day, March 2, I visited the Presidential Palace, also known as La Casa Rosada (the Pink House), an elegant structure in the Spanish Rococo style. I was shown into President Carlos Menem's office, where he was waiting. An impressive chandelier enhanced the stately ambience of the room.

President Menem, who continued in office for ten years after our encounter, had been elected in July the previous year (1989). He spoke with me of his mentor, the late President Juan Perón, recalling him warmly as one dedicated to the education and development of young people. He said that Perón served as inspiration for him and the youth of his generation, even through the lengthy years of the leader's exile. It was President Menem's resolve to carry on in the spirit of his mentor.

He then presented the Order of Merit of May in the Grade of Grand Cross, in honor of my father's contributions to world peace and the welfare of humanity. "May" in the name of this award refers to the May Revolution, which established Argentina's independence from Spain in 1810. The honor is of the highest order, bestowed upon international figures of distinguished achievement and service.

After returning to Japan, I placed the medal in front of our family altar and recited the sutra together with my parents. I will never forget the quiet observation my mother then made, "This is an award essentially honoring all the SGI members in Argentina; it really is a testament to their achievements."

Whenever I have traveled overseas on my father's behalf, my

mother chants Nam-myoho-renge-kyo with a prayer for my success, day or night, whatever the time.

■ ■ ■ ■ ■

My father returned to Japan from the United States the day I accepted the Argentine medal, on March 2. One cold and rainy spring morning, thinking of his friends in Argentina amid the South American summer heat, he composed for them a long poem, part of which reads:

> *Ah,*
> *If only my wishes had wings,*
> *That I could fly to the beautiful "Land of Silver"*
> *Still yet unseen*
> *Where the fragrant red flower ceibo blooms,*
> *Argentina, vast land of light*
> *I deeply regret*
> *that my visit could not be.*
> *Still, someday I will surely go—*
> *I will pray, and await the time*
> *Each day like a thousand—no, ten thousand, autumns*
> *Until the day I set foot in the land of Argentina!*

True to his words, my father made his first visit to Argentina three years later, in February 1993, as part of a tour to five South American countries (including Colombia, Brazil, Paraguay and Chile). During that trip, he visited his fiftieth country.

Published August 23, 2000

8

An Art Exhibition in Spain, Land Rich in Culture

"You want the Tokyo Fuji Art Museum to put on a Western art exhibition in Spain?" I asked this question in surprise to Dr. Ricardo Díez-Hochleitner, a friend of my father and also president of the Club of Rome,[1] who had just proposed the exhibition be brought to Spain, his homeland, as I escorted him on a tour of the Tokyo Fuji Art Museum.

Spain is a country that brings to mind great figures of the art world: the sixteenth-century master El Greco; Velázquez of the seventeenth century; Goya in the eighteenth; and Picasso, Dali and Miró of the twentieth century. The capital, Madrid, is home to a host of art museums of prominence, including one of the world's most renowned, the Museo del Prado.

I questioned the impact of a Japanese museum putting on an exhibition of Western art in Spain, a great European country so steeped in art and culture. But Dr. Díez-Hochleitner insisted, "An exquisite collection such as this is rarely seen even in Europe." To display these works in Spain, he said, where expectations are high, would attest to the breadth and caliber of the Tokyo Fuji Art Museum.

My father, the founder of the Tokyo Fuji Art Museum, saw this as an important opportunity for cultural exchange between the two countries and fully endorsed it. Detailed planning for the exhibition got under way at once.

In June 1995, with the cooperation of the Santillana Foundation—for which Dr. Díez-Hochleitner served as vice president—works from the Tokyo Fuji Art Museum were showcased in an exhibition called "French Impressionism: Symphony of Light and Color" at the Foundation's gallery in Santillana del Mar, a small village in northern Spain. Visitors from all over Europe come to this historic town, its cobblestone streets lined with stone houses and courtyards unchanged since medieval times.

The exhibition opened in grand style with many honored guests attending, including then Spanish Minister of Culture Carmen Alborch Bataller. I attended on my father's behalf. The media covered the event widely—an indicator of the nation's appreciation of the arts. Observing all of this, I realized that Dr. Díez-Hochleitner's idea had been on the mark.

■ ■ ■ ■ ■

Bullfighting and flamenco popularly symbolize the courage and passion of Spain. It has been my impression that the country emerged as a world power out of grand-scale pursuits and an indomitable spirit of enterprise. At one time it vied with its neighbor Portugal to control half the globe. The Spanish empire, however, eventually waned, its once innovative policies outmoded and its visionary worldview lost, making it possible for the emerging powers of England and France to overtake it as a global presence. Clearly, imperial illusions that sprang from arrogance and conceit took their toll. It can be said that no society, organization or individual is immune to such weaknesses.

The capital, Madrid, is nestled in the great plateau of central Spain. As our delegation flew over the region, the lush green city suddenly came into view amid the bare, reddish-brown highlands. I remember that when my father first visited Madrid, in 1961, the city impressed him as somewhat cheerless and desolate. Returning twenty-two years later, in 1983, he found it a metropolis abundant with life and energy. One significant change that had occurred in Spain during that span of time was the enthronement of King Juan Carlos I in 1975. The ascendance to the throne of the thirty-seven-year-old monarch signaled the sunset of fascism and the dawn of democracy. In connection with the Tokyo Fuji Art Museum's "French Impressionism" exhibition, my father had intended to make his third visit to Spain in 1995. Both the king and my father were honorary members of the Club of Rome, and so he had also planned to pay the king a courtesy visit. But his trip could not be realized.

At the same time the "French Impressionism" exhibition was being held in Madrid, a Japanese performing arts event sponsored by the Min-On Concert Association[2] took place in Santander, a seaport on Spain's north coast. Rich in cultural influences from around the world, Santander can be described as an intellectual crossroad on the sea, at which artists and scholars converge and exchange ideas. The City of Santander presented my father its Distinguished Service Award for his efforts in widely promoting grassroots cultural exchange. The award presentation took place at the Magdalena Palace. Standing high on a small peninsula, the palace was once the summer retreat of the Spanish Royal Family. It is now the headquarters of an international university, a palace of culture playing host to academic conferences and summer courses.

El Ateneo de Santander, a prestigious cultural and educational association in Santander founded in 1914, takes great pride in its heritage. At the association's invitation, I presented my father's lecture titled "Toward the Dawn of Twenty-first-Century Civilization," which seemed to resonate well with the audience of some two hundred cultural leaders, including Dr. Díez-Hochleitner. Essentially, the lecture addressed this point: When people's inherent virtues begin to shine—giving rise to progress and creativity, the readiness to take on challenges and to break new ground, self-reliance and initiative—then civilization, too, will shine.

■ ■ ■ ■ ■

In February 1998, my father finally was able to meet King Juan Carlos I of Spain at a gathering of the Order of the Knights of Rizal in the Philippines, once a Spanish colony. My father presented the king with a poem he had composed, "Al Gran Rey de la Paz, sol de España" (To the great king of peace, the sun of Spain). A passage from that poem reads:

> *At one time, Spain*
> *brought about the encounter of two civilizations,*
> *the New World and the Old World,*
> *uniting our round world into a single destiny.*
> *The five hundred years that followed*
> *saw the intermingling of countless joys and sorrows—*
> *but in the next five hundred years,*

the great hope for the unification of mankind created a new era, a "civilization of communication," the dawn of a new "golden century."

In just a few short weeks, we will greet the dawn of the twenty-first century, aware that it is we who must lead in actualizing humanity's great hopes for the future.

Published November 22, 2000

NOTES

1. Club of Rome—In April 1968, an international group of professionals from the fields of diplomacy, industry, academia and civil society met at a quiet villa in Rome. Invited by Italian industrialist Aurelio Peccei and Scottish scientist Alexander King, they came together to discuss the dilemma of prevailing short-term thinking in international affairs and, in particular, the concerns regarding unlimited resource consumption in an increasingly interdependent world. Dr. Ricardo Díez-Hochleitner was president of the Club of Rome from 1991 to 2000. See http://www.clubofrome.org
2. Min-On Concert Association promotes and hosts diverse musical performances around the world with the aim of bringing together people of different cultures. The association was founded in 1963 by Daisaku Ikeda, and its activities include exchanges, competitions, festivals and concerts.

9

In Guangzhou, China: My Father's 100th Academic Honor

WHEN I MET Lin Shusen, mayor of Guangzhou, China, on February 14, 2001, he said to me with great energy and confidence: "I understand that when President Ikeda first visited China, he passed through Guangzhou on his way to Beijing. At that time, Guangzhou was just a small city, but things have changed considerably since then!" I had gone to Guangzhou on my father's behalf to accept an honorary citizenship awarded him by the city.

Guangzhou, the capital of Guangdong Province in southern China, has a population of close to ten million and ranks with Beijing and Shanghai as one of China's largest cities. With an average annual temperature of sixty-eight degrees Fahrenheit and a humid subtropical climate, Guangzhou has gained the nickname "Flower City," because flowers bloom there year-round.

The Pearl River, which runs through the center of the city and flows into the South China Sea, for more than two thousand years was the starting point of the so-called Silk Road of the Sea, the Ocean route that linked China to Southeast Asia and India. European powers invaded Guangzhou in the nineteenth century, and Japanese forces occupied it during the Sino-Japanese War of 1937–1945. Dr. Sun Yat-sen, the father of the Chinese Revolution, made Guangzhou the seat of his activities. There he founded Zhongshan University, also known as Sun Yat-sen University, which conferred an honorary professorship on my father in 1996.

Indeed, Guangzhou has grown remarkably during the last ten years, the government's policy of economic reforms contributing to its rapid development. Seeing Guangzhou with its bristling skyscrapers for the first time, I found the city much larger than I had imagined. Incidentally, Guangzhou is famous for its Cantonese cuisine. "Guangzhou is where the food is," a popular saying goes. Given the renown of its native fare, I was surprised to find a Japanese sushi bar there.

■ ■ ■ ■ ■

Nowadays the flight from Tokyo to Beijing takes only four hours. When my father first visited China, in 1974, there were no direct flights to Beijing. From Hong Kong, he walked across the bridge at Shenzhen, which spanned the border between Hong Kong and mainland China, took a train to Guangzhou, and there boarded a plane to Beijing. A university student at the time, I remember reading the detailed account of my father's trip in the *Seikyo Shimbun*, the Soka Gakkai's daily newspaper, as well as my excitement at witnessing the start of a new era of friendship between Japan and China. Ten years later, in 1984, I had the opportunity to visit China with a delegation from the social studies department of Soka High School. We toured part of the Silk Road, traveling by way of Xi'an to Dunhuang (famed for its caves filled with Buddhist art) and on to Urumqi. I recalled the route that Buddhism had traveled, coming to China from India via the Silk Road, and then spreading to the Korean Peninsula before finally making its way to Japan. Again I was reminded of the great debt we Japanese owe to China for its role in bringing Buddhism to us. And yet, when the People's Republic of China was established after World War II, the Japanese government viewed it, in the context of the Cold War, as an enemy state. There was virtually no public sentiment in Japan calling for friendly relations with our neighbor China.

Nevertheless, at the 11th Soka Gakkai Student Division General Meeting in 1968, my father called for the normalization of diplomatic relations between Japan and China. He presented a similar argument in volume 5 of his historical novel *The Human Revolution*, published the following year. His efforts during that time did much to bolster the courage and hope of anyone who wished for harmonious relations between the two countries. Then, in 1971, Komeito (Clean Government Party) representatives visited China with the intent of fostering diplomatic ties.

■ ■ ■ ■ ■

Just before my visit to Guangzhou on February 11, 2001, I attended an SGI-Hong Kong event, the New Century Hong Kong Youth Culture Festival. That day would have marked the 101st birthday of Josei Toda, the second Soka Gakkai president. Also on that day, volume 9 of *The New Human Revolution* was published in Japan. That volume recounts the 1964 founding of Komeito. It makes clear that while the Soka Gakkai is supportive of Komeito, the party independently formulates its own policies and principles. As the party's founder, however, my father did make one request: that Komeito work to restore Japan's diplomatic relations with China.

On February 16, the month and day of Nichiren Daishonin's birth, the Guangdong Province Academy of Social Sciences awarded my father an honorary professorship, which I accepted on his behalf at a conferral ceremony held at the academy's campus in Guangzhou. The Guangdong Province Academy of Social Sciences, established in 1958, has become one of the top research institutions in the province. Often referred to as the brain trust behind China's economic liberalization, its researchers continue to shape social, economic and political policies that can lead the China of the new century.

With the academy's designation of honorary professor, the number of academic titles conferred on my father from institutions of higher learning reached one hundred. In the twenty-six years since his first honorary doctorate, from Moscow State University in 1975, institutions in thirty-six countries and territories spanning five continents have conferred on him such awards.[1] I trust that these honors will serve as a source of pride for students and graduates of Soka Schools and SGI members around the world.

In his acceptance speech, which I read at the ceremony, my father noted that it is the mission and destiny of our generation to establish a path to peace and prosperity, one that will endure for not only one or two hundred years, but for a thousand or even ten thousand years to come.

■ ■ ■ ■ ■

This brings to mind the meeting in December 1974 between Prime Minister Zhou Enlai of China, then seventy-six and in declining health, and my father, who was forty-six at the time. The premier conveyed his expectations that my father strive to develop a people's network of peace, and said to him: "You are a young man, so the time we spend together is of vital importance. These last twenty-five years of the twentieth century are the most important for the world as a whole."

True to the promise he made to Premier Zhou, my father has traveled the world, opening the way for a spiritual Silk Road through cultural and educational exchanges. And now—so quickly, it seems—my father has surpassed the age of the premier when they met. To realize a path to peace and prosperity that will last thousands or tens of thousands of years, I feel it is up to us to choose and steadfastly carry on this mission of our predecessors—the mission to create a spiritual Silk Road for humanity.

Published March 14, 2001

Notes

1. As of July 2008, there have been more than 240 academic titles conferred upon SGI President Daisaku Ikeda from institutions of higher learning throughout the world.

10

India, the Birthplace of Buddhism

At a Soka Gakkai Headquarters leaders meeting in July 2002, my father introduced a *tanka*, or short poem, that second Soka Gakkai president Josei Toda had composed fifty years earlier:

> *Now, let us set out on a journey*
> *Our hearts emboldened*
> *To spread the Mystic Law*
> *To the farthest reaches*
> *Of the Land of the Moon.*[1]

Land of the Moon is an ancient name for India used in China and Japan.

In July 1951, a year before Mr. Toda composed this poem, the young men's division was established. At a ceremony marking that occasion, President Toda addressed the gathering of more than one hundred young men, saying: "The next president of the Soka Gakkai will without doubt appear from among those present here today. I believe he is here. I wish to express my deepest respect and heartfelt congratulations to him. . . . Our objective is not so narrow as to be limited in scope to just the one country of Japan. Nichiren Daishonin decreed that we spread the Great Pure Law to Korea, China and as far as India. Indeed, we must accomplish *kosen-rufu*[2] of Asia. If my life should end before that day comes, you must carry this out as my last wish. Accomplish this goal, whatever may happen."

My father was present at this gathering and later recorded in his diary his desire to go to India, the birthplace of Buddhism, as soon as would be possible.[3] In February 1961, the year after he became the third Soka Gakkai president, he visited India for the first time. Very few Soka Gakkai members lived in India at the time. That visit represented the first step toward the "*kosen-rufu* of Asia," and the seeds for the spread of the Mystic Law in India had now been securely planted.

■ ■ ■ ■ ■

In January 1988, I made my first trip to India, to accept on my father's behalf the Dr. G. Ramachandran Award for International Understanding. This was my father's first award of recognition arising from India. On January 4, two days after his sixtieth birthday, I set out from Japan and arrived at the airport in New Delhi at two o'clock in the morning on January 5. Gandhigram Rural University, where the presentation ceremony was to be held, is located just outside of Madurai in Southern India. Getting there from New Delhi required several connecting flights, bringing my entire journey to more than twenty-four hours.

A distinguished disciple of Mahatma Gandhi, Dr. G. Ramachandran served for many years as a driving force behind the nonviolence movement of India and later founded Gandhigram Rural University. Despite his venerable age of eighty-two, Dr. Ramachandran spoke with great vigor at the presentation ceremony about his hopes for peace. He looked to the youth of both India and Japan as duty-bound to initiate a new movement for nonviolence and peace. Dr. Ramachandran died in 1995, and so my father never had the opportunity to speak with him directly. His spirit, however, clearly lives on in the friendship and dialogue between his disciple, Dr. N. Radhakrishnan (former Director of the Gandhi Memorial Museum), and my father.

I visited India again in December 1990 and had the great fortune to meet Rajiv Gandhi, who was the grandson of India's first prime minister, Jawaharlal Nehru, and son of India's second prime minister, Indira Gandhi. Rajiv Gandhi himself became prime minister after his mother's assassination in 1984. A year later, in November 1985, he visited Japan and met with my father at the State Guesthouse in Tokyo. Mr. Gandhi lost reelection as prime minister in 1989, but at the time I met him I was told he was certain to win the next election and regain the post.

On arrival at Mr. Gandhi's private residence in New Delhi, our delegation underwent a thorough security inspection, which included a check underneath our vehicle. I was aware, of course, that Mr. Gandhi's mother had been assassinated, but the level of security was sobering and gave me a sense of the dangers surrounding him.

The residence waiting room was packed with visitors. When it came my turn to see him, the first thing Mr. Gandhi said to me was: "I remember well my meeting with the SGI president five years ago. I would really like to visit Soka University during my next trip to Japan." He seemed genuinely excited about this, and there was a warm air of familiarity about him, though it was the first time we had met.

When I spoke of my father's proposed "King Ashoka, Mahatma Gandhi and Nehru" exhibition, which at that time I was charged with organizing, I recall Mr. Gandhi generously saying to me: "India and Japan, through mutual cooperation, can be great leaders in the world. Both countries have a tradition of creatively harmonizing old cultures and customs with modern technology, yet without compromising the human element. This exhibition will be of great value to the friendship of our two nations. I will be more than happy to cooperate with you on this project."

Unfortunately, six months later, in May 1991, Mr. Gandhi, while campaigning for reelection, was assassinated by a suicide bomber. Nine months after his sudden death, in February 1992, my parents and I met with his widow, Sonia Gandhi, in the same room where I had spoken with her husband two years earlier.

"In life, there are many storms and dark nights that one must get through," my father said to her. "The stormier and darker the night, the brighter the morning of happiness that awaits you. You must transform fate into value and change destiny into mission while looking forward, always forward. That is the teaching of India's native son Shakyamuni Buddha."[4] Mrs. Gandhi, who until that moment had maintained a stern expression, nodded and smiled. I will never forget her smile.

■ ■ ■ ■ ■

Mrs. Gandhi and her daughter, Priyanka, came to Japan in October 1994 to attend the opening ceremony of the "King

Ashoka, Mahatma Gandhi and Jawaharlal Nehru—The Healing Touch" exhibition at the Tokyo Fuji Art Museum. In the course of conversation, it came up that photography had been a favorite hobby of Rajiv Gandhi. My father suggested that we honor his life by holding an exhibition of the late prime minister's photographic works. His family agreed, and Priyanka took the lead in the project, from the selection of photos to the exhibition's design. In 1996, the "Rajiv Gandhi: An Intimate Vision" photographic exhibition was put on display in five Japanese cities, including Tokyo.

The following year, I attended the grand opening of the exhibition in New Delhi with my parents. In the exhibition hall hung a photo of my father meeting with Rajiv Gandhi. Then, near day's end, as if to celebrate the opening, a spectacular double rainbow graced the evening sky.

Earlier that day, I had visited the Soka Bodhi Tree Garden, about an hour's car ride south of New Delhi. From the road on the way, I could see cows, camels and elephants. As I arrived at the garden, the expansiveness of the grounds struck me. Lush and green, with a variety of trees and flowers, it stretched as far as the eye could see. Shakyamuni Buddha is said to have attained enlightenment while sitting in meditation under a *bodhi* tree. It had been my father's idea to create a garden of such trees in the birthplace of the teachings of Buddhism, and SGI members have played key roles in maintaining the beautiful landscape.

Inside the garden's Friendship Hall Center is a monument inscribed with another *tanka* poem by President Toda:

> *To the people of Asia*
> *who pray for a glimpse of the moon,*
> *through the parting clouds,*

let us send, instead,
the light of the sun.[5]

Shakyamuni Buddha appeared in India, the Land of the Moon, some three thousand years ago. He taught Buddhism, which later spread to China, the Korean Peninsula and Japan. The time had come for Nichiren Buddhism—the Buddhism of the sun—to shine brightly upon India and all of Asia. This, I believe, is the sentiment President Toda expresses in his poem.

In Nichiren's words: "The moon appears in the west and sheds its light eastward, but the sun rises in the east and casts its rays to the west. The same is true of Buddhism."[6] In accord with this teaching, President Toda made a solemn vow to spread Buddhism throughout Asia, and left it to my father, his disciple, to actualize its westward return through that continent. In the summer of 2002, India's prestigious Himachal Pradesh University conferred on my father an honorary doctorate of literature. The occasion also marked the fifty-fifth anniversary of my father's first encounter with President Toda. It was his seventh academic honor from an Indian university and one hundred thirtieth such crown of intellect from a world university.[7] We should never forget that the Buddhist philosophy of peace and culture has spread to 183 countries and territories throughout the world because of the spirit of the disciple to realize the mentor's vision.[8]

Published September 11, 2002

Notes

1. Daisaku Ikeda, *The Human Revolution* (Santa Monica, CA: World Tribune Press, 2004), p. 1969.
2. *Kosen-rufu*—A term drawn from the Lotus Sutra that literally means to declare and spread widely; Nichiren interpreted this to mean widely propagating the teaching of Nam-myoho-renge-kyo, which he identified as the essence of the sutra. The "Medicine King" (twenty-third) chapter of the Lotus Sutra reads, "After I [Shakyamuni Buddha] have passed into extinction, in the last five-hundred-year period you must spread it abroad widely (*kosen-rufu*) throughout Jambudvipa and never allow it to be cut off." In the SGI *kosen-rufu* is used to indicate the establishment of a peaceful world based on the humane principles of Buddhism.
3. Daisaku Ikeda, *A Youthful Diary: One Man's Journey From the Beginning of Faith to Worldwide Leadership for Peace* (Santa Monica, CA: World Tribune Press, 2000), p. 339.
4. See *The Writings of Nichiren Daishonin*, vol. 2 (Tokyo: Soka Gakkai, 2006), pp. 741–44, and March–April 2008 *Living Buddhism* (Santa Monica, CA: SGI-USA Publications, 2008), pp. 69–72.
5. Daisaku Ikeda, *The New Human Revolution*, vol. 13 (Santa Monica, CA: World Tribune Press, 2000), p. 5.
6. *The Writings of Nichiren Daishonin*, vol. 1 (Tokyo: Soka Gakkai, 1999), p. 401.
7. As of July 2008, there have been more than 240 academic titles conferred upon SGI President Daisaku Ikeda from institutions of higher learning throughout the world.
8. As of August 24, 2008, the SGI's movement for peace, culture and education has spread to 192 countries and territories around the world.

11

Pioneers of Brazil

WE ARE now (in June 2002) at the height of the World Cup soccer tournament, hosted this year by South Korea and Japan. To experience at such close range this major sports event—one that comes only once every four years—I think will be memorable for all. This brings to mind my trip in June 1998 to Brazil, a country known as the "land of soccer," when the World Cup was being held in France.

I was in São Paulo the day the Brazilian team played. The game was to begin that evening—a weeknight—and I remember the city streets being jammed with traffic as people left work early to get home in time to watch it on television. Those of us visiting from Japan could do nothing but remain in our hotel rooms and, like everyone else, watch the game. We were told that, at a time like this, even dogs and cats stay indoors.

As the game began, an unusual silence fell over the city. And when Brazil scored a goal, the entire city, it seemed, erupted in cheers as the sound of firecrackers echoed in the streets. That was my firsthand experience of Brazil's overwhelming passion for soccer.

The purpose of my visit was to attend a festival commemorating the ninetieth anniversary of the first Japanese immigrants to arrive in Brazil. On April 28, 1908, the ship *Kasato Maru* set sail from Japan's Port of Kobe with 781 passengers. After a fifty-two day voyage, it finally docked at Port Santos in Brazil on June 18. Since then, immigrants and second- and third-generation Japanese Brazilians have weathered two world wars and other periods of hardship to become the world's largest ethnic Japanese community outside of Japan, today numbering more than one million.

Brazilian parliamentarian Antonio Ueno, a friend of my father, had chaired the executive committee for the ninetieth anniversary festival held in Paraná on June 20. The state of Paraná is home to a large Japanese community. Thirty thousand ethnic Japanese gathered for the event under a huge tent set up at an agricultural center in the countryside.

With President Fernando Henrique Cardoso attending, on everyone's mind was whether he would announce his candidacy for reelection. Perhaps the enthusiastic response of the audience encouraged the president, because he told them, "I am looking forward to attending the one-hundredth anniversary, ten years from now, as your president." Thunderous applause arose from the crowd.

Keizo Obuchi, Japan's minister of foreign affairs at the time, spoke next and announced, "I would also like to attend the one-hundredth anniversary, as Prime Minister of Japan." Coincidently, three weeks later, Japan's Liberal Democratic Party unexpectedly lost the House of Councilors election, forcing Prime Minister Ryutaro Hashimoto to step down. Replacing him as Prime Minister was Keizo Obuchi.

Performances by seven hundred members of the Brazil SGI

youth division were a highlight of the day's events. In Brazil, individual performance and skill are strongly emphasized, even in team sports such as soccer. And so the Brazil SGI Brass Band, Fife and Drum Corps and gymnastics team amazed the crowd with their formations and precision group movement. They also impressed President Cardoso, who, while applauding, said to me: "This is wonderful. I am so happy to see that there are youth like these in my country. They are the hope of Brazil!"

■ ■ ■ ■ ■

This festival is a national event in Brazil that celebrates the pioneering spirit of immigrants. The eightieth-anniversary festival, in 1988, took place at an outdoor stadium in São Paulo where ten thousand Brazil SGI members performed card stunts.[1] The audience of eighty thousand included the president of Brazil and members of the Imperial Family of Japan. The fact that Brazil SGI was invited to take a leading role in a national event of this importance signifies the level of trust it had gained from society. There had been a time, however, when the organization was labeled dangerous and closely scrutinized by the government.

During my father's second trip to Brazil in 1966, federal police kept him and his group under surveillance. At the culture festival held by the Brazil association of the Soka Gakkai, lines of police closely monitored the attendees as they entered the venue. The government—a military dictatorship that seized power in a coup d'état two years before—and police believed allegations in the local media that painted the Soka Gakkai as a dangerous group with ties to communists.

Eight years later, in March 1974, my father was planning to travel to Brazil after visiting the United States. He was denied entry into Brazil, however, on the suspicion that the Soka Gakkai was a communist organization. Citing my father's visit to China in May and to the Soviet Union in September that year, Brazilian media later reported that "the Soka Gakkai is indeed communist."

The members in Brazil felt it their responsibility to dispel these misunderstandings and prejudice. Based on the principle that Buddhism finds expression in society, they took it upon themselves to find ways of contributing to their communities. They resolved to create the circumstances in which the president of Brazil would someday personally invite SGI President Ikeda to visit their country. And finally, in 1984, thanks to just such an invitation from President João Baptista de Oliveira Figueiredo, my father made his third visit to Brazil, his first in eighteen years.

■ ■ ■ ■ ■

My first trip to Brazil was unanticipated. While in the United States in February 1990, I received a sudden request to visit three South American countries on my father's behalf. On that trip, I attended the opening of the "Treasures of Japanese Art" exhibition (from the Tokyo Fuji Art Museum collection) at Brazil's foremost art museum, the São Paulo Museum of Art. Brazilians of Japanese descent were excited at this first major exhibition of Japanese art in their country, and ethnic Brazilians responded enthusiastically, as well. A positive contribution had clearly been made to strengthening friendly relations between Japan and Brazil.

Two years later, in 1992, I visited Brazil again, this time for the debut of "Dialogue With Nature," an exhibition of my father's photographs, at the same museum. During that visit I was honored to meet Dr. Austregésilo de Athayde, president of the Brazilian Academy of Letters.[2] Dr. Athayde, then ninety-three, was frail and could barely walk on his own. Yet he extended his withered hand to me with a vibrant twinkle in his eye. With a powerful handshake, he told me: "I would most certainly like to meet your father. Please give him my regards." In February 1993, Dr. Athayde and my father met in Rio de Janeiro, at which time my father was appointed an overseas member of the Academy, making him the first Japanese national among the members of the Academy.

To this day, Brazil SGI continues to be an exemplary organization in our global movement. There are more than twenty state and city streets, parks and bridges named after the Soka Gakkai's three founding presidents. Among them: Tsunesaburo Makiguchi Street, Josei Toda Park and Dr. Daisaku Ikeda Environmental Park. Brazil SGI has overcome the suspicion and prejudice once fueled by some Japanese religious groups in Brazil. The organization has wholly won the trust of Brazil's Japanese community and has come to play a prominent role in every Japanese immigration festival. Seeing the growth of the Brazil SGI youth makes me happiest of all. On my first visit to Brazil, a culture festival performance put on by the BSGI high school division members was impressive. The current young men's division leader and young women's division leader were among the members of the high school division at that time.

The pioneering spirit of the first Japanese immigrants to Brazil has been passed on for more than ninety years. Today, the young generation of Brazil SGI members steadily carry it on as the pioneering spirit of *kosen-rufu*, the spirit to work for the happiness of all people.

Published June 26, 2002

Notes

1. Card stunts—An audience participation performance in which each person in a section of seating is given a set of cards and raises a specific card in response to a cue. The result is the instantaneous creation of images or words across the entire section, creating a striking effect when viewed at a distance.
2. Brazilian Academy of Letters (Academia Brasilia)—A nonprofit established in the 1800s in Brazil, inspired by the Académie Française. The Academia Brasilia is the official authority on the national language of Brazil, Portuguese. From its inception, the academy consisted of forty members, known as "immortals," chosen from among citizens of Brazil who have published recognized works of literary value.

12

The Opening of Soka University of America in Aliso Viejo, California

On August 17, 2002, Soka University of America welcomed its second class of undergraduate students to its campus in Aliso Viejo, California. The previous year, I attended the entrance ceremony and shared my good wishes with the students. Unlike universities in Japan, American universities, I understand, don't usually hold entrance ceremonies for incoming students. I suppose that it is because, in America, greater emphasis is placed on doing one's best after entering college than on simply being accepted. That being the case, the entrance ceremony at SUA,[1] at which many people gather to celebrate and to offer the new students their best wishes, may well be the grandest such ceremony in the United States.

Above the stage at the first entrance ceremony, in August 2001, hung a banner that read "Welcome Class of 2005." I was particularly impressed by a statement one professor made in his address to the students. He commented that the fun would end with the entrance ceremony, and from the next day, the students would be expected to devote themselves to their studies and work hard to graduate in 2005.

Since the opening of Soka University in Japan (1971), it had been my father's long-cherished wish to establish a university in the United States. As a first step, in 1987, the Los Angeles campus of Soka University—formerly known as Soka University Los Angeles (SULA)— opened as a branch campus of Soka University in Japan in Calabasas, California, a community on the outskirts of that city. The property, with its charming buildings of Spanish architecture set amid lush natural surroundings, had been developed and maintained by a number of landowners over the course of many decades. Not far from the entertainment studios of Hollywood, it often was used as a filming location for movies, television programs and commercials. The final scene from the movie classic *Gone With the Wind* was filmed along the tree-lined road leading into the campus.

Study-abroad language programs for students of Soka University, Soka Women's College and Soka Schools in Japan were initiated at this campus. Through the program, participants developed a global outlook, and many came to play active roles in the international community, furthering the values and application of Soka education. Plans were announced in 1990 to open a full-fledged university at the site. Because of the location's natural beauty, however, several environmental groups and others opposed this plan, proposing instead that the property be designated national parkland.

In response, the school commissioned environmental impact studies, established the Botanical Research Center and Nursery, and facilitated a series of community meetings with local residents to communicate the university's resolve to protect the environment. Efforts were also made to convey the spirit and intent behind establishing Soka University in the United States: to foster promising and talented young people who would contribute positively to American society and to the world at large. In addition, the university organized a human rights lecture series, inviting several prominent representatives of the American civil rights movement as speakers. They included Rosa Parks, known as the mother of the civil rights movement, and Coretta Scott King, the widow of Dr. Martin Luther King Jr.

In America, people tend to support a cause once convinced of its merit. Some who at first opposed the Los Angeles campus gradually became its strong supporters, to the extent that a number of local residents formed a group called Friends of Soka. In addition, the university coordinated its efforts with the Los Angeles-based Simon Wiesenthal Center, an influential Jewish human rights institution. The Wiesenthal Center sponsored exhibitions titled "The Courage to Remember—Anne Frank and the Holocaust" and "Friedl and the Children of Terezín," both of which were very well received in California and in Japan.

The Soka University campus in Calabasas was also the venue for my father's encounters with the world-renowned astronomer Dr. Robert Jastrow and with two-time Nobel Laureate Dr. Linus Pauling. His meeting with Dr. Jastrow led to the development of relations between Kansai Soka Schools and the Mount Wilson Observatory, near Los Angeles, as well as the National Aeronautics and Space Administration. The encounter with Dr. Pauling became an impetus for the "Linus Pauling and the Twentieth Century: Quest for Humanity" exhibition that is touring Japan this year (2002).

In 1992, the Soka University campus in Calabasas began to offer the public a variety of educational programs.[2] These included Spanish-language courses as well as Japanese-language instruction through the campus's Japanese Language Center, which opened in 1993. In 1994, when the campus received degree-granting approval from the Bureau for Private Postsecondary and Vocational Education (BPPVE) for the State of California, SULA's name was changed to Soka University of America, distinguishing it as a freestanding independent institution separate from Soka University in Japan. The Graduate School was established in 1994, offering a Master of Arts degree in Second and Foreign Language Education with a concentration in Teaching English to Speakers of Other Languages (TESOL). It has accepted students from all over the world, many of whom are today applying the skills they gained at SUA in their respective homelands.

As Soka University of America continued to develop trust in the community and expand its operations, one day, in 1994, administrators received a propitious phone call. It was a representative of a major landowner and development firm: "We are well aware of your efforts [to establish your university]. We own property ready for development in an area where the local residents would welcome you with open arms. How would you feel about constructing a campus there?"

The property is located atop a hill abutting the large and growing residential community of Aliso Viejo in Orange County, California. It is surrounded by a park on 80 percent of its borders, and beyond the hills at the far end of the wilderness park stretches the Pacific Ocean. The Aliso Viejo campus is now the site of SUA.[3]

My father introduced the plan for establishing the Aliso Viejo campus the following year (1995), at the graduation ceremony of Soka University in Japan. Without delay, in July, Orange County delivered a resolution welcoming the university. Construction began in 1997, and the campus opened in 2001, the first year of the new millennium. That year was also the thirtieth anniversary of the founding of Soka University in Japan and the one-hundredth anniversary of the birth of Tsunesaburo Makiguchi, the father of Soka education.

The school's Dedication Ceremony took place on May 3, 2001, the start of the Soka Gakkai's second set of Seven Bells.[4] Congratulatory telegrams from US President George W. Bush, former president of the Soviet Union Mikhail Gorbachev and more than one hundred universities worldwide honored the event. In August the following year, the Graduate School of Soka University of America (SUA) in Calabasas welcomed its ninth class.

At a community lecture delivered as part of the Dedication Ceremony (on May 4, 2001), Dr. Lawrence Edward Carter Sr. of Morehouse College spoke of the university saying that SUA is already a prestigious university of world-renown due to its founder.

SUA is truly a university of the people, the product of the sincerity of many in responding to the founder's passion for education. And along with its founder, Daisaku Ikeda, people worldwide are praying daily for the school's development and its students' growth. In this sense, it is a university unmatched the world over. From here on, its value will be determined by the degree to which its graduates flourish and contribute actively to society.

> *Be philosophers of a renaissance of life.*
> *Be world citizens in solidarity for peace.*
> *Be the pioneers of a global civilization.*

I think that these three mottoes of SUA will surely resonate with any young person today. Those who apply and embody these mottoes are genuine leaders of peace, culture and humanity in the twenty-first century.

Published August 28, 2002

Notes

1. Soka University of America held entrance ceremonies during the first four years of its undergraduate program, as there was not yet a class to graduate. With the graduation of the first entering class in 2005, SUA no longer held entrance ceremonies and instead focused on the annual commencement ceremony held at the end of the academic year. Since then, its first-year students participate in orientation and a special welcome reception at the beginning of the year.
2. In 1992, the Soka University, Calabasas campus initiated the Human Rights Lecture Series, bringing a variety of speakers to the campus. In 1993, the Botanical Center and the Japanese Language Center opened, and the Pan Pacific Business Seminar series was initiated to educate local entrepreneurs on doing business in the Pacific Rim.
3. In 2007, the Soka University, Calabasas campus closed and the graduate program moved to the Aliso Viejo campus, uniting both programs on one campus for the first time.
4. The Seven Bells—Successive seven-year periods that have marked the Soka Gakkai's advancement since its founding on November 18, 1930. In his December 13, 2000, address, SGI President Ikeda announced that May 3, 2001, would mark the start of the second set of Seven Bells, signaling the start of a new cycle in the SGI's history. May 3, 2001, the fiftieth anniversary of Josei Toda becoming the second Soka Gakkai president, was the dedication date of the Soka University of America, Aliso Viejo campus. The goal of the second set of Seven Bells (2001–2050) is to secure the foundation for peace in Asia and throughout the world.

13

A Shared Peace: Cultural and Educational Exchange With Mongolia

THE 2002 sumo wrestling season in Japan concluded with the Kyushu Grand Sumo Tournament, at which grand champion Asashoryu, a native of Mongolia, captured his first Emperor's Cup. The year also marks the thirtieth anniversary of diplomatic relations between Japan and Mongolia. Asashoryu's first championship victory opens a new page in the story of friendship between the two countries.

On November 20, while the Kyushu tournament was under way, Mongolia's Shikhikhutug Law School conferred an honorary doctorate on my father. The most famous figure that comes to mind in connection with Mongolia is Genghis Khan, the thirteenth-century conqueror and founder of the Mongol Empire. Few are aware, however, that one of his ministers, a legal expert named Shikhikhutug, was largely responsible for developing the empire into a political power.

In modern times, sandwiched between the socialist giants Soviet Russia and China, Mongolia became a socialist republic.

Amid the wave of democratization that followed the dissolution of the Soviet Union in 1991, Mongolia instituted a multiparty political system. In 1992, it established a new constitution that called for a parliamentary democracy and completely transformed its legal system. Shikhikhutug Law School, founded in 1991, became the nation's first private law school. Many of its graduates have become lawyers, prosecutors and judges—capable legal professionals making important contributions to the development of a new Mongolia.

■ ■ ■ ■ ■

Japan and Mongolia both have histories that span some two thousand years. In all that time, the two countries encountered each other in a significant way only on two occasions. The first was the so-called Yuan Incursion, the Mongol invasions of Japan in the thirteenth century; the other, known as the Nomonhan Incident, took place in the twentieth century.

Nichiren Daishonin was born in the final years of the life of Genghis Khan, the founder and first ruler of the Mongol Empire. Genghis' grandson, Kublai, sent emissaries to Japan to demand tribute to the Empire, but the government in Kamakura refused. Because of that, the great Mongol army twice besieged the city of Hakata on Japan's southernmost major island of Kyushu. In Japan, these invasions are known as the Yuan Incursion because Kublai Khan had named his Mongol administration in China the Yuan Dynasty.

In fact, the Kamakura government beheaded the five Mongol emissaries who had been sent to Japan at the execution grounds of Tatsunokuchi, near Kamakura. This happened four years after government officials had attempted to behead Nichiren at the same spot, in 1271, in what became known as the Tatsunokuchi Persecution. Denouncing the government's execution of the emissaries, Nichiren writes, "It is indeed a pity that… the innocent Mongol envoys have been beheaded."[1] And: "How pitiful that Hei no Saemon and the lord of Sagami failed to heed me! If they had, they would surely not have beheaded the envoys from the Mongol empire who arrived a few years ago."[2]

Nichiren also relates a transcendent Buddhist view of these events, "The nation may be devastated by the superior strength of the Mongols, but the slander of the correct teaching will cease almost entirely."[3] In another letter, he further explains, "Therefore, Brahma, Shakra, the gods of the sun and moon, and the four heavenly kings have taken possession of the body of the Mongol ruler and are causing him to chastise our nation."[4]

The second historical encounter between Japan and Mongolia, the Nomonhan Incident, was a conflict sparked by a border dispute that took place in 1939, during the Sino-Japanese War. In Nomonhan, a town on the border between Mongolia and Japanese-controlled Manchuria, Japanese soldiers opened fire on Soviet and Mongolian troops. This sparked a nearly four-month-long battle that ended in the complete devastation of the Japanese forces. In Mongolia and Russia, the conflict is known as the Battle of Khalkhin Gol (named after the Khalkhin River).

■ ■ ■ ■ ■

My father wrote a short story that is set in Mongolia, titled *The Great Prairie and the White Horse*. It appeared as a series in the *Shogakusei Bunka Shimbun* (Elementary Students' Cultural News), the newspaper of the Soka Gakkai elementary school division, and was then published as a book in 1999. In the story's epilogue, he shares some thoughts on Mongolia: "I remember President Toda saying to me, 'Daisaku, I would like to ride with you across the Mongolian plains on horseback!' —The vast blue sky! The broad green plain! The hearts of the people, broader still! Across that Mongolian countryside gallops Bator (the story's main character). With the steppes of Mongolia as a setting, I wanted someday to express in writing the way of living that President Toda taught me: To remain undefeated, no matter what hardships may come."

The book was translated into the Mongolian language by Rector Tsedev of the Mongolian University of Arts and Culture, and published in Mongolia in 2000.

I recall reading with great excitement as a high school student Yasushi Inoue's book *Aoki ookami* (The Blue Wolf), about a young boy named Temujin of the Mongolian plains who grows up to be the great Genghis Khan. I also remember reading, around the same time, the mystery novel *Chingisuhaan no himitsu* (The Secrets of Genghis Khan). In the story, the legendary samurai general Minamoto Yoshitsune,[5] who was believed to have died at Hiraizumi in northern Japan, survives and crosses over into mainland Asia to become Genghis Khan.

One of my Japanese history textbooks touched on an interesting theory, which traced the origin of the Japanese people to the conquest of Japan by horse-mounted nomads. According to this theory, a nomadic tribe from the Asian Steppes migrated southward through the Korean Peninsula, crossing into Japan and conquering it in the fourth or fifth century. In any event, Mongolia remained in my imagination a vast and mysterious land, romantic and dreamlike.

The author (back left) with his parents and brother, Takahiro. Karuizawa, Nagano, Japan, August 1997.

The Ikeda family (author, back left). Tokyo, 1967.

At Kobayashi-cho in Ota Ward, with mother and brothers (author, far right). Tokyo, 1961.

Flowering cherry trees near the Tokyo-Ota Ikeda Culture Center in Ota Ward, Tokyo, where the author once lived with his family.

SGI President Ikeda writing *The Human Revolution* at the Seikyo Shimbun building in Shinano-machi, Tokyo, 1971.

Visiting a bookstore with SGI President Ikeda (author is at center). Books Otori, Koenji Branch, in Suginami, Tokyo, December 1970.

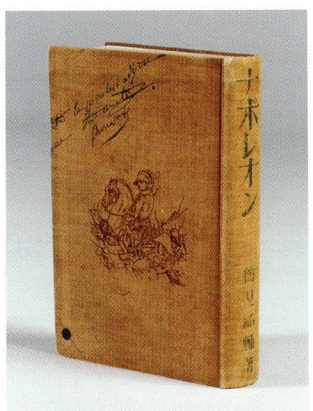 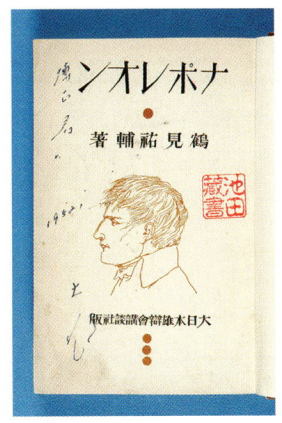

(Left) *Napoleon*, published August 5, 1931, given to the author by SGI President Ikeda.
(Right) Inside cover of *Napoleon*. Written on the left side in the youthful handwriting of SGI President Ikeda: "To my dear Hiromasa, from Daisaku."

"There is a person whom I must endeavor to meet even if it shortens my life," Premier Zhou Enlai (second from left) stated. Despite declining health, he meets with SGI President Ikeda. Beijing, China, December 1974.

The author meets with former Soviet Premier Mikhail Gorbachev (right). Gorbachev Foundation Headquarters in Moscow, May 2000.

(Left to right): The author; Priyanka Gandhi Vadra, Sonia Gandhi's daughter; Mrs. Kaneko Ikeda; Sonia Gandhi, widow of the late Indian Prime Minister Rajiv Gandhi; SGI President Ikeda; Robert Vadra, Priyanka's husband; and Takahiro Ikeda, the author's younger brother. The photo hung at back left is of the late Prime Minister Rajiv Gandhi. Sonia Gandhi's residence in New Delhi, India, October 1997.

The author accepted an honorary doctorate on behalf of SGI President Ikeda at the University of Buenos Aires, one of the foremost universities in South America. (Above) He delivers the SGI president's acceptance speech. The university rector, Dr. Oscar Shuberoff (center). University Main Building, March 1990.

The author with Brazilian President Fernando Cardoso (center), applauding the performance of the SGI-Brazil youth division at the Japanese Immigration Festival commemorating the ninetieth year of the Japanese immigration to Brazil. The Agricultural Center of Rolandia outside of Londrina, June 1998.

The author meets with Dr. Austregésilo de Athayde, president of the Brazilian Academy of Letters. Rio de Janeiro, January 1992.

The author at the Paris showing of "Dialogue With Nature," an exhibition of photographs by Daisaku Ikeda, with Alain Poher of the French Senate (left) and René Huyghe (right). Jacquemart-André Museum, May 1988.

Miyazaki, Japan, March 1999. Photo taken by SGI President Ikeda.

Dedication of Gandhi Hall, named for Mahatma M. K. Gandhi, the leader of the nonviolence movement. From right to left: SUA President Daniel Habuki; the author; Orange County Chairman of the Board of Supervisors Thomas W. Wilson; Dr. Arun Gandhi (Mahatma Gandhi's grandson) and his wife, Sunanda Gandhi; and Aliso Viejo Mayor Carmen Vali. Soka University of America, Aliso Viejo campus, August 2001.

The author (far right) unveils a memorial plaque inscribed with second Soka Gakkai president Josei Toda's poem in the Bharat Soka Gakkai Ikeda Friendship Center at the Soka Bodhi Tree Garden, New Delhi, India. Dr. N. Radhakrishnan (second from right) is the former director of the Gandhi Memorial Museum. India, October 1997.

At the United Kingdom's prestigious University of Glasgow on the occasion of SGI President Ikeda receiving an honorary doctorate. (Left to right): The author; Mrs. Kaneko Ikeda; Professor J. Forbes Munro, Clerk of the Senate at the University of Glasgow; President Ikeda; and Takahiro Ikeda. University of Glasgow campus, June 1994.

The author accepts an honorary doctorate in education on behalf of SGI President Ikeda from South Africa's University of the North. University Auditorium, Transvaal, South Africa, September 1995.

(Left to right): The author with Jordan's Prince El Hassan bin Talal; Dr. Lawrence E. Carter Sr., Dean of Morehouse College's Martin Luther King Jr. International Chapel; and Morehouse College President Walter E. Massey as they unveil a portrait of SGI President Ikeda and Mrs. Ikeda. The portrait is now displayed in the Heroes of Civil Rights Sanctuary at the Martin Luther King Jr. International Chapel, Morehouse College in Atlanta, Georgia. Morehouse College, August 2001.

The "Gandhi, King, Ikeda—A Legacy of Building Peace" exhibition opens in Japan at Soka University, Hachioji, Tokyo, September 2002. This exhibition has now been held in the United States, Canada, India and other countries, to tremendous popular acclaim.

The final showing of the "Linus Pauling and the Twentieth Century" exhibition in Japan at the Soka University Administration Building. Dr. Linus Pauling Jr. gave the opening address. At far left is a bust of Dr. Linus Pauling. Hachioji, Tokyo, October 2002.

The Soka Schools founder (center) takes the starter's pistol during the 4th Fitness Day / Founder's Cup Marathon Event at the Kansai Soka Schools. Author is in the foreground. Osaka, Japan, October 1985.

Kansai Soka High School, where the author taught from 1978 to 1988.

A joint graduation ceremony for students from Tokyo Soka High School, Soka Elementary School and Soka Women's College. The students, together with the founder, express their hopes in accord with the ideal of the school song "Kusaki wa moyuru." Hakucho Gymnasium at Soka Women's College in Hachioji, Tokyo, January 2003.

SGI President Ikeda receives the Mahatma M. K. Gandhi Millennium Award from the Mahatma Gandhi Foundation for Non-violent Peace, at the Year 2000 School of the Future Assembly. Soka University Auditorium, Hachioji, Tokyo, September 2000.

The characters for the university's name carved in the monument at Soka University's front gate are in first Soka Gakkai president Tsunesaburo Makiguchi's calligraphy. Hachioji, Tokyo.

Soka University of America in Aliso Viejo, California. The university's mission is to foster a steady stream of global citizens committed to living a contributive life.

The Soka University of America founder, Daisaku Ikeda, and Mrs. Kaneko Ikeda with SUA student representatives of the second undergraduate class, the class of 2006. Soka University, Hachioji, Tokyo, April 2002.

The author addresses the audience at the first Entrance Ceremony of Soka University of America. Soka University of America, Aliso Viejo campus, August 2001.

SGI President Ikeda is awarded an honorary doctorate in philosophy, and his wife, Kaneko, an honorary doctorate in law from Chinese Culture University of Taiwan. Soka University Administration Building, Hachioji, Tokyo, March 2003.

SGI President Ikeda takes up his pen for his friends, for the future.

The Long Walk in Windsor, United Kingdom, June 1991. Photo taken by SGI President Ikeda.

Although of similar Asian roots, the peoples of Mongolia and Japan have had limited contact, and Mongolia for most Japanese is a land they've only dreamed of. Following Mongolia's democratization in the 1990s, however, brisk exchange between the two nations began. My father has had a number of discussions with Mongolia's cultural and intellectual leaders, beginning in 1993 with Nambaryn Enkhbayar, then the Minister of Culture. In 1998, my father and I met with the president of Mongolia, Natsagiin Bagabandi, during his visit to Japan. While in Japan, the Mongolian leader visited Soka University and delivered a lecture there. In 2001, eight years after my father first met him, Mr. Enkhbayar became prime minister, and when he visited Japan, they met again.

In 1996, the SGI World Boys and Girls Art Exhibition opened in the Mongolian capital, Ulaanbaatar, and my father's photography exhibition "Dialogue With Nature" appeared there in 1997. The Mongolian National Ensemble of Folk Song and Dance performed in Japan in 1994 and 1996. In July this year (2002), near the town of Nomonhan, where the two countries share an unhappy history, the Ikeda Peace Park opened to commemorate the thirtieth anniversary of diplomatic relations between Mongolia and Japan. In the park's center stands a monument engraved with a passage, in both Japanese and Mongolian, from the opening of my father's historical novel *The New Human Revolution*: "Nothing is more precious than peace. Nothing brings more happiness. Peace is the most basic starting point for the advancement of humankind."[6] Mongolia has a land mass four times that of Japan. Of its population of just over two million,

70 percent is under age thirty-five, making Mongolia truly a nation of youth. It is the youth of our two nations who will fill, with culture and education, the gaps in our previously unfortunate history and create a new history of shared peace.

Published December 11, 2002

Notes

1. *The Writings of Nichiren Daishonin*, vol. 1, p. 628.
2. *The Writings of Nichiren Daishonin*, vol. 1, p. 845.
3. *The Writings of Nichiren Daishonin*, vol. 1, p. 618.
4. *The Writings of Nichiren Daishonin*, vol. 1, pp. 530–31.
5. Minamoto Yoshitsune (1159–1189)—A general of the Minamoto clan of Japan, whose tactics won a string of victories that partly led to the establishment of the Kamakura shogunate in 1192 under Minamoto Yoritomo, Yoshitsune's half-brother. This marked the rise of military (samurai) power and the suppression of the emperor's power. (Four great clans dominated Japanese politics during the Heian period (794–1185)—the Fujiwara, the Minamoto, the Taira and the Tachibana.)
6. Daisaku Ikeda, *The New Human Revolution*, vol. 1 (Santa Monica, CA: World Tribune Press, 1995), p. 1.

Toward the Century
of Human Revolution

14

Hiroshima: Shaping the Spirit of Humanity

MY FATHER wrote a short novel titled *Journey to Hiroshima*, about a junior high school student named Kazushiro who spends a summer at his aunt's home in Hiroshima. There he gains a deep sense of the tragedy wrought by the atomic bombing of that city. The story was serialized in the *Chugakusei bunka shimbun* (Junior High School Students' Cultural News), the Soka Gakkai Junior High School Division's newspaper, beginning in August 1986.

August 6 this year (2001) marked the fifty-sixth anniversary of the atomic bombing of Hiroshima. In remembrance of that day, a dialogue between Nuclear Age Peace Foundation President David Krieger and my father was published in English under the title *Choose Hope*. Their dialogue, I believe, sheds light on ways to achieve the important goal set forth in the declaration read at the City of Hiroshima Peace Memorial Ceremony: "We, the citizens of Hiroshima, living witnesses to 'the century of war,' hereby declare that we will do everything in our power to make the twenty-first century one of peace and humanity, free from nuclear weapons."[1]

My father and Dr. Krieger have met on three occasions, the first in 1997. Having been present at their exchanges, I was most impressed by Dr. Krieger's affable nature and his ever-present smile. We first met him at the Soka Gakkai's World Youth Peace Music Festival in Yokohama, held to commemorate the fortieth anniversary of President Toda's Declaration for the Abolition of Nuclear Weapons.[2] During the festival, Dr. Krieger presented us with sunflower seeds as a symbolic gesture of peace. He explained that the gift expressed his desire to eliminate nuclear arms worldwide and have sunflowers bloom where weapons manufacturing facilities are shut down. Because the goal of abolition is formidable, anti-nuclear arms movements can tend toward an unreachable idealism, and so I was impressed with Dr. Krieger's idea of planting sunflowers—a tangible act—to gauge his progress.

Dr. Krieger took his first step as a pacifist at age twenty-one, after visiting Hiroshima and Nagasaki. As an American, he said, he learned in school that "the bombings of Hiroshima and Nagasaki were necessary to win the war. . . . We bombed these two cities and the war ended, therefore the bomb was a good thing."[3] Until he visited those two cities, however, he had not realized that the bombings "were basically attacks against civilian populations."[4] He told us that visiting the sites and, for the first time, seeing photographs of the bombed-out streets and charred corpses shocked him beyond words.

My first visit to Nagasaki was with a school field trip while in my third year of junior high school. On the tour of the Nagasaki Atomic Bomb Museum, we saw displays of photographs and personal items of the victims. This left a deep impression, something that has stayed with me.

In one of his meetings with Dr. Krieger, my father mentioned that he had been educated under Japan's militarist system. To this, Dr. Krieger replied: "Young people lack a reference point with which to judge the education they receive. . . . A culture that infuses education with nationalism and militarism is a failed culture."[5]

The ideology of nationalism holds the country to be more important than its people and one's own national identity to be superior to that of others. Geographically separated from other countries, the Japanese people are said to have developed an island-nation mentality, to be quick to criticize cultures different from their own. It is crucial, however, to learn to view other cultures without prejudice, to appreciate them as they are. I believe it important to avoid judging anyone based on limited personal experience or immediate emotional impression.

My father is a long-standing advocate of the right to education—education that is humanistic and immune to political control. To this view, education exists for the good of humankind rather than the political interests of a particular state. It would be wrong to allow nationalistic political aims to interfere with the educational process. In other words, education is not a tool of the state; it is a function of both state and society to support education.

Dr. Krieger makes the point that "if enough young people were educated to think for themselves about fighting, killing and the value of life, we would be well on our way toward a peaceful world."[6] I believe that his words express the essential purpose that education must aim to fulfill.

■ ■ ■ ■ ■

In *Choose Hope*, the book title of the dialogue between Dr. Krieger and my father, the word *hope*, I feel, conveys the boundless trust and expectation these two place in young people. In March 2000, my father, accompanied by Dr. Krieger, attended a Soka Schools graduation, and in his address said: "The power of hope exists within the lives of all people. Where there is no hope, you should create it. To lose hope is foolish; after all, creating hope is a uniquely human capacity. In any situation, we must move toward peace, move toward hope, and be determined to create value—that is the essence of Soka."

As my father said, hope comes from within, and so the best course lies in the strengthening of our hearts and minds. The path of Soka, of value creation, exists for this purpose.

In *Journey to Hiroshima*, as Kazushiro's summer vacation comes to an end, his aunt shares with him a quote that makes him realize the importance of building a strong mind. It is a passage from the philosopher Michel de Montaigne: "Neither good nor ill is done to us by Fortune: she merely offers us the matter and the seeds: our soul, more powerful than she is, can mould it or sow them as she pleases, being the only cause and mistress of our happy state or our unhappiness."[7] In life, we at times experience hardship and pain. We encounter setbacks and sometimes overwhelming despair. But these things are all building material for the self. Whether we choose to wallow in unhappiness or stand fast and use our ordeals as springboards toward happiness: this depends on one thing—whether we are strong and unbeatable at heart.

The path to abolishing nuclear weapons is a difficult one. Unless we act with courage, the world will veer inevitably toward its own destruction. Humanity has the option to choose despair, but by choosing hope, and only by choosing hope, can we begin to create a better world. What hope we have depends on what we value. Rather than a hope that aims for small things and focuses only on self-interest, we must seek from within a vast and noble hope, one that transcends the ego to embrace all humanity.

The New Human Revolution, my father's serialized novel about the development of the SGI, will consist of thirty volumes when completed. This series, which began on August 6, 1993, the forty-eighth anniversary of the atomic bombing of Hiroshima, opens with the lines: "Nothing is more precious than peace. Nothing brings more happiness. Peace is the most basic starting point for the advancement of humankind."[8] The fact that he wrote that passage on the anniversary of the Hiroshima bombing, I feel, conveys his strong resolve and commitment to realizing peace. The spirit of Hiroshima—the spirit to rid the world of nuclear weapons—is something we must strive to make the spirit of all humanity. In doing so, we shape the twenty-first century into a century of peace.

Published August 22, 2001

Notes

1. *Japan Weekly Monitor*, August 13, 2001; IPGF web page, http://www.ipgf.org/hiroshima.asp
2. On September 8, 1957, Josei Toda made his Declaration for the Abolition of Nuclear Weapons to fifty thousand people during the Soka Gakkai's fourth East Japan Athletic Meet at the Mitsuzawa Athletic Stadium in Yokohama.
3. David Krieger and Daisaku Ikeda, *Choose Hope* (Santa Monica, CA: Middleway Press, 2002), p. 74.
4. *Choose Hope*, p. 74.
5. *Choose Hope*, p. 57.
6. *Choose Hope*, p. 58.
7. Screech, M.A., *The Complete Essays*, trans. Michel de Montaigne, (London: Penguin Books, 2003), (I:14) 71.

8. Daisaku Ikeda, *The New Human Revolution*, vol. 1 (Santa Monica, CA: World Tribune Press, 1995), p. 1.

15

The Human Power of Peace

This January 26, 2001, SGI Day, I attended a meeting of the young women's division international group. There I spoke about the SGI president's annual peace proposal, "Creating and Sustaining a Century of Life: Challenges for a New Era," which had just been published in Japanese. When I returned to the Soka Gakkai Headquarters after the meeting, the day's news was being broadcast on television. The top story related a tragedy that had occurred in Tokyo, at Shin-Okubo Station on the Yamanote train line: A man had fallen from a station platform onto the tracks, and he and two other men—who had tried to save him—were struck and killed by a train.

A little after eleven that night at the Soka Gakkai Headquarters, we received a phone call from Vice Chairman Akashi Ouchi of Bharat Soka Gakkai in India. Mr. Ouchi is a lifelong Soka Gakkai member originally from Shinjuku, Tokyo. In his youthful days, he drew inspiration from the high school division's motto "Young Phoenixes, Take Flight into the Future," and made a determination to contribute to the growth of Nichiren

Buddhism in India. He called now from India to let us know that there had been a major earthquake in the western part of the country. My father inquired after and confirmed the safety of the SGI members there, and sent a telegram to the president of India expressing his sympathy and support.

These two sad events, both occurring on January 26, moved me to think deeply about the meaning of humane action and behavior.

■ ■ ■ ■ ■

In August 1971, my father spent the entire month at the head temple Taiseki-ji to encourage ten thousand members attending summer courses there. For one, the high school division had a three-day and two-night session that began on August 4. I was a senior at the time and participated in the program with nearly seven thousand other high school students from all around the country.

While our summer courses were taking place, the Boy Scouts were holding their World Jamboree[1] at nearby Asagiri Heights. More than twenty thousand boys from eighty-nine countries participated in this grand camping event. Unfortunately, a storm spawned by a passing typhoon unleashed a massive downpour on the campgrounds. Tents were flooded, and sixty-five hundred of the boys were evacuated to safe ground at Taiseki-ji.

What unfolded then is still vivid to me. I remember closely observing my father at the evacuation operations center in the first floor lobby of the Grand Lecture Hall, as scores of people hurried in and out. He spent hours directing the relief operation, quickly giving specific directions in response to each matter that arose. To welcome and cheer up the rain-soaked boys, he instructed that a bonfire be lit and that the youth division Brass Band and Fife and Drum Corps be assembled to perform. He also saw to the boys' immediate needs with blankets, towels, bread, rice balls and other relief supplies. Members of the high school division's language committee even took on the role of impromptu interpreters.[2]

At one point, someone expressed reluctance to allow the boys into the Gohonzon room of the Grand Lecture Hall, because they were covered up to their knees in mud. But my father countered: "The spirit of Buddhism is to extend a hand to those who are suffering. Right now it is more important to take care of these people in need than the floors and *tatami* mats. We can always have the floors cleaned and replace the *tatami* later if necessary."[3] Amidst the trying circumstances, he calmly attended to every unexpected situation that arose.

Although these events took place during just one night, they provided opportunities to encounter people of the same generation from around the globe and develop friendships across borders, ethnicity and religion. Today, many of the youth who participated in that World Jamboree have become prominent figures in their countries. In my encounters with people around the world, there have been times when someone tells me, out of the blue, "I was at that Jamboree when you helped us out." I suppose that for anyone who has received help in a time of distress, the memory of that experience lasts a lifetime.

■ ■ ■ ■ ■

The courage of the two men who sacrificed their lives—one a Korean exchange student and the other a Japanese photographer—while trying to save the man at Shin-Okubo Station moved many people. And in the aftermath of the major earthquake that struck India, Bharat Soka Gakkai sprang into action by supplying relief goods and deploying medical teams and other humanitarian support. In Japan, fund-raising campaigns to aid in the relief effort also got under way.

In his 2001 peace proposal, my father contends that the way forward in the twenty-first century is to restore a worldview based on what Buddhism terms dependent origination. The Chinese character translated as "dependent" means that all things are linked by causal relationships. My father expresses the hope that each person develops fortitude, that is, inner spiritual resources of self-mastery. Humane action requires the strength of heart and spirit to embrace a worldview that recognizes that all life exists amid a web of interconnection. Indifference and apathy, he points out, only encourage evil and lead to confusion and destruction.

The SGI movement is awakening this spirit of humanism throughout the world. As of today, there are people of such spiritual fortitude in 163 countries and territories around the world.[4] Each SGI member, as a good and trusted citizen, is engaging in open dialogue along the daily course of life, developing ties of friendship among many people. Is this not the essence of the current of humanity that will make the twenty-first century a century of life?

■ ■ ■ ■ ■

The great Indian earthquake of 2001 struck Gujarat, the state in western India that is the birthplace of Mahatma Gandhi, who once said that if ten million people join the peace movement of nonviolence, it can unsettle any authority. Unfortunately, an assassin's bullet ended his life on January 30, 1948. Ten years later, on February 10, 1958, the eve of his own last birthday, President Toda told my father: "It will be an incredible time when there are ten million practitioners of Nichiren Buddhism. It is exciting, really very exciting." Developing a membership of ten million in Japan was President Toda's ultimate wish, and I believe it will lead to creating the foundation for the unwavering power of peace in the twenty-first century.

The second set of Seven Bells[5] begins in 2001 and ends in 2050. It is up to youth to lead in realizing President Toda's vision of a foundation for world peace in the first fifty years of the twenty-first century.

Published February 14, 2001

Notes

1. The World Jamboree is a festival at which Boy Scouts from throughout the globe come together to foster mutual understanding and friendship. The event mentioned here was the first of its kind to be held in Japan. See Daisaku Ikeda, *The New Human Revolution*, vol. 15 (Santa Monica, CA: World Tribune Press, 2008), p. 317.
2. Daisaku Ikeda, *The New Human Revolution*, vol. 15 (Santa Monica, CA: World Tribune Press, 2008), p. 322.
3. *The New Human Revolution*, vol. 15, p. 325.
4. As of August 24, 2008, the SGI's movement for peace, culture and education has spread to 192 countries and territories around the world.
5. Second set of Seven Bells—The start of a new cycle in the SGI's history, beginning on May 3, 2001, the fiftieth anniversary of Josei Toda becoming the second Soka Gakkai president and the dedication date of the Soka University of America, Aliso Viejo campus. The goal of the second set of Seven Bells (2001–2050) is to secure the foundation for peace in Asia and throughout the world. See Chapter 12 notes for an explanation of the SGI's first set of Seven Bells.

16

The Oneness of Mentor and Disciple: Our Founding Spirit

NOVEMBER 18 marks the anniversary of the Soka Gakkai's founding. On this date in 1930, Tsunesaburo Makiguchi, who would become the organization's first president, published the first volume of his work *Soka kyoikugaku taikei* (The System of Value-Creating Pedagogy). The book's imprint reads, "Author: Tsunesaburo Makiguchi; Publisher: Jogai [later, Josei] Toda; Publishing Office: Soka Kyoiku Gakkai." The name *Soka* had been made known to the world for the first time, and the date of the publication later came to be recognized as the date of the Soka Gakkai's founding.[1] No ceremony or meeting was held, and only two people participated in this founding event: the fifty-nine-year-old mentor and his thirty-year-old disciple. Their passionate will and fearless struggle arising from their spirit of oneness as mentor and disciple became the source of the Soka Gakkai's remarkable and continuing growth.

November 18 is significant for another reason. On that date in 1944, President Makiguchi died in prison. During the war,

Japan's militarist regime attempted to impose the state-sanctioned religion, Shinto, on all its citizens, a policy that President Makiguchi, based on his convictions as a Buddhist, strenuously opposed. As a result, authorities arrested and imprisoned him on charges of lèse majesté and violating the Peace Preservation Law.[2] President Makiguchi nonetheless continued to uphold his beliefs throughout the ordeal and, after one year and four months of incarceration, died in jail a martyr at seventy-three.

The founding of the Soka Schools also took place on November 18.[3] This signifies the founder's hope that we will carry on President Makiguchi's enduring wish to establish Soka education. In addition, April 2, the anniversary of President Toda's passing, marks the founding of Soka University in Japan. The honoring of these two dates by the Soka educational system expresses its founder's deeply held wish that future generations inherit the spirit of his mentor, President Toda, and President Toda's mentor, President Makiguchi.

Soka University and Soka Schools essentially began with the formation of the Soka University Establishment Steering Committee in November 1965. My father, at age thirty-seven, chaired the committee. Fifteen years had passed since President Toda first told him of his dream to establish a university.

By November 1950, troubles with President Toda's businesses had become so serious that he was not able to pay his employees. One day, while he and my father were having lunch together at a university cafeteria near his office, President Toda said: "President Makiguchi always spoke of his desire to create a school based on his vision. Tragically forced to end his days while in prison, he did not see his dream realized. I am sure that is something he regretted. As President Makiguchi's disciple entrusted with fulfilling his vision, I have always sworn to build a school on his behalf. I wish that I could accomplish this while I am still alive and well, but that may not happen. If that's the case, I am counting on you. Let's make it the best university in the world!"

Half a century after President Toda entrusted my father with creating "the best university in the world," Soka University stands today as a world-class institution in every sense.

■ ■ ■ ■ ■

The events that led to the founding of Soka Schools are described in the chapter "Glorious Future" of *The New Human Revolution*, volume 12, now (in November 2001) being serialized in the *Seikyo Shimbun*. When the first class entered Soka Schools in 1968, I was in my third year of junior high school. At the time, I had no sense of the convictions that lay behind my father's efforts to found Soka Schools. Age-wise, I could have entered the second class of Soka High School and, later, Soka University, but I continued in the school system I was currently in, which included my junior high school through college. As a result, I did not experience Soka education as a student. But in the years that followed, I took part as an educator, and for that opportunity I am extremely grateful.

Nowadays, Soka graduates, including some of my former students, are working in the Soka educational system. I am extremely happy to see that Soka schooling has today become a solid educational tradition. My hope is to enroll someday in the Soka University correspondence program and thereby eventually become an alumnus.

"Once you become aware of your great mission to spread your wings and soar into the future, your abilities will quickly expand." This is one of my favorite sayings, a point my father emphasized at the 1st High School Division General Meeting held the summer of the year that Soka Schools opened. It means that those who become determined to fulfill their mission for *kosen-rufu*—humanity's most noble objective—will as a result come to display their innate abilities to the fullest. In addition to Soka Schools and Soka University in Japan, Soka University of America now presents another option for students who wish to pursue Soka education. To make the possibilities inherent in these choices a reality, there is no other way but to work hard, applying the abilities you have gained by awakening to your mission.

■ ■ ■ ■

We must never forget the significance of another event that occurred in our founding month of November. On November 28, 1991, the Nichiren Shoshu priesthood, without dialogue or discussion, excommunicated the Soka Gakkai in Japan and the SGI worldwide. The priesthood, having orchestrated a series of attacks on the Soka Gakkai, must have thought that expulsion would lead to our organization's decline, but this scheme failed entirely. Contrary to the priests' designs, the Soka Gakkai is now stronger than ever. At the time of its excommunication, the Soka Gakkai International had a presence in 115 countries and territories worldwide; ten years later that number grew to 177 countries and territories.[4]

As another testament to growth and progress, in 1992, following the opening of the Hong Kong Soka Kindergarten, the Soka educational system was established in Singapore, Malaysia and this year (2001) in Brazil. In the United States, the Graduate

School of Soka University of America opened in 1994. Talented students with a profound sense of mission gathered there from around the world in their quest for Soka education.

In the span of ten years since the excommunication, the number of academic honors my father had received from institutions of higher learning worldwide came to exactly one hundred.[5] Interestingly enough, an honorary professorship (his 112th academic honor) from Guangzhou University in China was awarded to my father on November 18, 2001.

As my father approached his seventieth birthday, he resolved that the foundations for humanity's peace and happiness—the groundwork he has laid for worldwide *kosen-rufu*—would be completed by the time he turned eighty. Next year, 2002, my father will turn seventy-four, surpassing the age of President Makiguchi.

In *The New Human Revolution*, my father writes: "True disciples are those who realize their mentor's ideals for the sake of *kosen-rufu*. The noble and great Buddhist path of the oneness of mentor and disciple is found only in such resolute action and victory."[6] The spirit of oneness between mentor and disciple lies at the core of Buddhism. The tremendous growth we have experienced until today is a testament to that spirit being passed on by our three founding presidents. We can take our founding month of November as an opportunity to study the history of the origins of the Soka Gakkai. As disciples, too, it is a time when we can renew our spirit of oneness with our mentor.

During the past several years, as each November 18 draws near, the Leonid meteors become a topic of conversation. The name *Leonid* derives from the star constellation Leo (the Lion) from which direction they appear to originate. On November 18, 2001, the meteor stream was the largest in several hundred years, turning the skies over the islands of Japan into a shower of light. I thought of it as the heavens sending their congratulations to the Soka Gakkai for its lion-like advances in our first founding month of the new century.

Published November 28, 2001

Notes

1. The Soka Kyoiku Gakkai (Value-Creating Education Society) was the forerunner of the Soka Gakkai and was founded by Tsunesaburo Makiguchi, who became its first president, and his disciple, Josei Toda, later its second president. Both were educators and converted to Nichiren Buddhism in 1928. At the time it was formed, the Soka Kyoiku Gakkai consisted principally of teachers and educators interested in Mr. Makiguchi's educational theories and practice. Its membership increased to some three thousand by the early 1940s. In July 1943, charged with violation of the Peace Preservation Law of 1925, and with lèse majesté against the emperor, Mr. Makiguchi and Mr. Toda were unjustly arrested and imprisoned. This was to suppress their activities to speak openly about Buddhist principles. Mr. Makiguchi died in prison in 1944, and Mr. Toda was released on parole on July 3, 1945. Amid a war-ravaged Japan, he set out to reconstruct the organization, renaming it the Soka Gakkai in 1946. His dropping of "Kyoiku," or "Education," from the name reflected the objective he envisioned for the organization to include people from and contribute to all fields and strata of society, transcending its role as a society of educators.
2. The Peace Preservation Law (*Chian-ijihô*) was passed in Japan in 1925 as a mechanism for the Imperial family to entrench itself against a growing left wing. It forbade conspiracy or revolt against the *kokutai*, or national essence, of Japan, and effectively criminalized socialism, communism and other ideologies that would threaten Japan's emperor-centered social order. In the late 1930s, this was extended to suppress the activities of religious groups. http://www.free-definition.com/Peace-Preservation-Law.html
3. The founding of the Soka Schools took place on November 18. The Soka Gakuen Educational Foundation was founded in November 1967, and Soka Junior and Senior High Schools in March 1968. www.soka.ed.jp/kyoiku/e_kyoiku/e_k0004.html

4. As of August 24, 2008, the SGI's movement for peace, culture and education has spread to 192 countries and territories around the world.
5. As of July 2008, there have been more than 240 academic titles conferred upon SGI President Daisaku Ikeda from institutions of higher learning throughout the world.
6. Daisaku Ikeda, *The New Human Revolution*, vol. 10 (Santa Monica, CA: World Tribune Press, 2004), p. 244.

17

Photographs From a Fully Engaged Life

THE OPENING ceremonies for the 2002 World Cup soccer championship, co-hosted by Japan and Korea, took place in Seoul on May 31, 2002. Meanwhile, "Dialogue With Nature," an exhibition of photographs taken by my father, was being shown at the Seoul Art Center. The exhibition ran for ten days and attracted some fifty thousand visitors.

Last June (2001), the Photographic Society of Malaysia awarded my father an honorary fellowship. In November, the Guangzhou Photographers Society named him its honorary president. And the Photographic Society of Singapore granted him an honorary lifetime membership.

My father is by no means a professional photographer. He does not bide his time looking for the perfect shot, nor does he own a sophisticated camera, nor has he ever studied advanced techniques of photography. Yet those who view his photographs have expressed wonder at his ability to capture inspiring images.

■ ■ ■ ■ ■

My father took up photography around 1970. The so-called Freedom of Speech Incident was at its boiling point, and he had fallen ill while working to resolve it. At that time, someone gave him a camera and suggested he try his hand at photography for a change of pace. Out of appreciation, he began taking photos with the intention of presenting some of them to the person who had given him the camera. Then, in June 1971, he found himself particularly moved by the beauty of the moon over Lake Ohnuma in Hokkaido and began snapping photos, taking as many as one hundred shots of that one scene.

While visiting Okinawa the following year, he presented his "Moon Over Onuma" photos as a gift to the Soka Gakkai members in Okinawa. They were framed and hung at the community center there, marking the first public display of his photographs. Learning of this, many other members spontaneously expressed their wish to have his photos on display at their local community centers as well, and in response my father endeavored to take photographs he hoped they would enjoy.

More than ten years after his start as a photographer, requests came for an exhibition of his photo collection. In April 1982, my father's first photography exhibition, "Dialogue With Nature," was displayed at the Fuji Art Museum in Shizuoka.

■ ■ ■ ■ ■

That same month, the Soka Schools became co-educational. The Tokyo campus, until then an all-boys school, began admitting girls, and the Kansai campus, until then an all-girls school, began admitting boys. As the teacher in charge of the first class of boys admitted to the Kansai campus, I approached my responsibility with equal measures of excitement and trepidation. René Huyghe, a member of the Académie Française, accompanied my father as a guest speaker at the entrance ceremony for this first co-ed class. He told the new students to keep their feet on the ground and their eyes on a hope-filled future. I, along with the students, found these words very encouraging.

I met Mr. Huyghe again six years later in Paris, in May 1988. He was then curator of the Jacquemart-André Museum, where I was to attend the opening of the "Dialogue With Nature" exhibition. Mr. Huyghe, a world-class art historian, praised my father's photographs as "poetry composed with the eye."

This was to be the first exhibition of my father's photography outside Japan. It seems Mr. Huyghe personally directed every aspect of the exhibition, from selecting the photographs, to their framing, to the actual display. Indeed, when I visited the gallery the day before the opening, I saw Mr. Huyghe giving careful instructions on finishing details such as the placement of the photos and the angle of lighting. Watching him work, I sensed his passionate commitment to bringing out the highest degree of artistic quality in my father's photos.

On opening day, among the many notable guests who came to view the exhibition were Alain Poher, president of the French Senate, who is a friend of my father, and curators Jan Wirgin of Sweden's National Museum of Far Eastern Antiquities and Jean Fage of France's Museum of Photography, whose institutions later hosted the exhibition in 1989 and 1990, respectively.

Paris is known as the birthplace of photography, and 1989 marked the one-hundred-fiftieth anniversary of the invention of the photographic process. That June, my father visited the French Museum of Photography in Bièvres, south of Paris, which named him an honorary staff member. In 1991 the Austrian artists association Künstlerhaus hailed his photo collection as an "outstanding achievement in artistic photography" and awarded him an honorary foreign-resident membership, making him the first Japanese citizen to receive the association's most prestigious honor.

France and Austria, two countries that epitomize European culture and art, were the first in the region to give artistic recognition to my father's photography. After the opening in Paris, the exhibition toured the world, appearing in eight cities and six countries throughout Europe, including Russia; seventeen cities in the United States, Canada and Mexico; seventeen cities in ten countries throughout Central and South America, including Brazil and Argentina; four cities in New Zealand and Australia of Oceania; and thirteen cities in six countries and territories of Asia, including Turkey and China. In August 2002, the exhibition traveled to Pusan, South Korea, bringing the total number of cities toured to sixty in twenty-seven countries and territories.[1]

The renowned German-born photographer and photographic historian Helmut Gernsheim said, "Photography is the only 'language' understood in all parts of the world, and bridging all nations and cultures, it links the family of man"(from Susan Sontag's *On Photography*).[2] "Dialogue With Nature," I feel, fulfills this role of a bridge linking nations and cultures.

■ ■ ■ ■ ■

On June 28, 2002, the day before the South Korean soccer team competed in the World Cup third-place playoff game in Seoul, the country's Sorabol College conferred on my father an honorary professorship at a ceremony held at the Seikyo Press building in Tokyo. Present at the ceremony, university founder Kim Il-Yoon observed: "I had the opportunity to view the photography exhibition in Seoul. I found myself wondering, how can such a busy person take such photographs? I then thought to myself that surely such photography could only be achieved by someone who has been fully and passionately engaged in life." My father has led a fully engaged and passionately devoted life, and this, I feel, is the reason his photos can touch the hearts of so many. And it is this, I have learned, not technique or knowledge, that truly moves people.

Published July 24, 2002

Notes

1. As of July 2008, the exhibition "Dialogue With Nature" has visited 124 cities in thirty-nine countries and regions.
2. Susan Sontag, *On Photography* (New York: Picador USA, 1973), p. 192.

18

Strong Ties With Ever-Victorious Kansai

Now that we are in the midst of summer vacation, many students may be reading books they did not have time to read during the school year. I remember being in high school and reading the novel *The Human Revolution*. Only six volumes had been published by then, and so I was able to read them straight through fairly quickly.

I had a love for history, so as I read the six volumes, I put together a simple chronology of the Soka Gakkai's development under the leadership of second Soka Gakkai president Josei Toda, along with events that unfolded in postwar Japanese society. It became the basis for a booklet I later created while teaching social studies at Kansai Soka Schools, "Postwar History Depicted in the Novel *The Human Revolution*." This chronology is still a helpful resource when I need to confirm events related to the Soka Gakkai's history. I find it encouraging that the reading I did during my high school years continues to serve a useful purpose decades later.

The complete set of *The Human Revolution* consists of twelve volumes, and as of today, ten volumes of *The New Human Revolution* have been published—a total of twenty-two volumes.[1] Reading them straight through would prove a daunting task. Nevertheless, I would encourage young people to start by just trying to read any part of any volume that seems to interest them.

■ ■ ■ ■ ■

In November 1978, the year I became a teacher at Kansai Soka Schools, volume 10 of *The Human Revolution* was published. That volume, set in the city of Osaka, depicts the campaign waged there by Shin'ichi Yamamoto in 1956.[2]

Whenever I attend Soka Gakkai meetings in the Osaka area, I almost always meet people who share their memories of that time. Some have told me that only after reading volume 10 did they gain a real sense of "Shin'ichi Yamamoto's" thoughts and feelings during that campaign.

I was only three years old in 1956 and, naturally, had not the slightest idea of where my father was or what he was doing at that time. Reading volume 10 of *The Human Revolution* while in Osaka, however, gave me some insight as to the origins of the strong bond between my father and the members in the Kansai region, where Osaka is located.

Volume 1 of *The Human Revolution* was published in 1965, and subsequent volumes, nearly every year thereafter, with each volume becoming a bestseller. But after volume 10, it would be more than a decade before publication of volume 11 was complete. Serialization of volume 11 began in the *Seikyo Shimbun* in August 1980, the year after my father's resignation as president of the Soka Gakkai.[3] Publication was discontinued, however, after the completion of three chapters—"Turning Point," "Stormy Days" and "Yubari."

The "Yubari" chapter depicts the Yubari Coal Miners Union Incident that occurred in the summer of 1957 in Hokkaido.[4] The final installment of the chapter has Shin'ichi Yamamoto, falsely accused of violating election laws, flying from Hokkaido's Chitose Airport to Osaka in order to turn himself in to the Osaka Prefectural Police. My father had planned to write about the Osaka Incident[5] in the next chapter, and Soka Gakkai members in the Kansai region, myself included, looked forward with great anticipation to reading it. Yet the series did not resume until 1991, ten years later. Finally, in January 1992, publication of volume 11 continued with two new chapters, "Osaka" and "Trial."

Truth be told, that period of more than ten years, during which the Soka Gakkai became the target of a number of malicious schemes, was a time of great turmoil for my father. At one point, he had to appear in court as a witness regarding crimes committed by Masatomo Yamazaki, who had been charged with extortion.[6] On another occasion, an illness sent my father to the hospital for the first time in his life.

It was during this period that I changed jobs from a teacher at Kansai Soka Schools to a member of the Soka Gakkai Headquarters staff in Tokyo.

The period of the Soka Gakkai's history between summer 1956 and autumn 1957 saw a series of challenging events, including the Yamaguchi Campaign,[7] the Yubari Coal Miners Union Incident and the Osaka Incident. In the postscript to volume 11, my father described it as "the greatest time of struggle" in his life. Yet, during the period he was writing volume 11, he also met with many fierce challenges.

The scenes portrayed in volume 9 of *The New Human Revolution* in the "Young Phoenixes" chapter overlap my own life experiences. That chapter describes events surrounding the establishment of the Soka Gakkai high school and junior high school divisions, including the junior high school division inaugural meeting, which I attended. Reading it not only brings back fond memories, it also gives me insight into the circumstances and events leading to the founding of the future division [collectively comprising members of the elementary, junior high and high school divisions].

■ ■ ■ ■ ■

The first work to bear the title *The Human Revolution* was a novel written by President Toda and serialized in the *Seikyo Shimbun*. The first installment appeared in the inaugural edition of that newspaper, on April 20, 1951. According to my father, Mr. Toda announced, "It's done!" and handed him the draft of the manuscript. Mr. Toda's novel was published as a book on July 3, 1957, the day my father flew from Hokkaido to Osaka. During a stopover at Haneda Airport in Tokyo, as my father prepared to catch the connecting flight to Osaka, President Toda met him and gave him a copy of the newly published book.

In that novel, President Makiguchi appears as the central character, and President Toda portrays himself as a character named Mr. Gan. My father told me that President Toda self-consciously remarked: "Although it was possible to portray President Makiguchi, it was quite another matter when it came to writing about myself. Embarrassment got the better of me."[8] Hearing this, my father resolved to write the continuation of *The Human Revolution* novel, focusing on President Toda's accomplishments. He records the intended theme in the preface: "A great human revolution in just a single individual will help achieve a change in the destiny of a nation, and further, will enable a change in the destiny of all humankind."

President Toda's pen name was Myo Goku, a play on words meant to bring to mind the character Songoku (Chinese, Sunwu Kong), the name of the monkey character in *Journey to the West*, one of the great works of Chinese literature. Myo Goku can be interpreted to signify Mr. Toda's awakening to *myo*, the wonderful principle that is the essence of Buddhism. My father's pen name is Ho Goku, the character *ho* indicating the dharma, or universal law. The two names together indicate *myoho*, the Mystic Law. In choosing the name *Ho Goku*, my father thus expressed his commitment as the disciple of President Toda.

The twelve volumes of Ho Goku's *The Human Revolution* ran as 1,509 installments in the *Seikyo Shimbun*. By August 2002, *The New Human Revolution* has been serialized through volume 13 in more than 2,250 installments. It is my hope that, during this summer vacation, young people will try to read one volume, or even just one chapter of *The Human Revolution*. I say this because I am confident that doing so will assist you in putting the principle of human revolution, the novel's main theme, into practice in your own life.

Published August 14, 2002

Notes

1. As of the publishing date of this book, twenty volumes in Japanese and fifteen volumes in English of *The New Human Revolution* have been published.
2. The author, SGI President Daisaku Ikeda, depicts himself as the character Shin'ichi Yamamoto in *The Human Revolution* and *The New Human Revolution*.

3. In 1979, Daisaku Ikeda resigned as president of the Soka Gakkai, and publication of volume 11 of *The Human Revolution* was postponed under pressure from the Nichiren Shoshu priesthood, which would not allow the Soka Gakkai to publish it.
4. Yubari Incident—During the summer of 1957, the Yubari Coal Miners Union, which supported the socialist parties, tried to exclude Soka Gakkai members on the basis of their support for their own candidate in the previous Upper House election.
5. Osaka Incident—In 1957, after a few Soka Gakkai members campaigning for candidates running for seats in the Upper House were caught violating election laws, authorities in Osaka, in an attempt to suppress the Soka Gakkai, falsely alleged that Daisaku Ikeda had orchestrated the illegal activities. After a four-and-a-half-year court case, Mr. Ikeda was fully acquitted.
6. Masatomo Yamazaki—The Soka Gakkai's first attorney, who was convicted of extortion against the organization in 1985 and imprisoned. Mr. Yamazaki was consistently ensnared in legal battles, often connected to attempts to use his relationship with the Soka Gakkai and with the Nichiren Shoshu priesthood to create schemes for his personal financial profit.
7. Yamaguchi Campaign—A propagation campaign in Yamaguchi Prefecture in October 1956 led by Daisaku Ikeda at the request of second Soka Gakkai president Josei Toda. The result was unprecedented. In four months, the membership increased tenfold from four hundred to four thousand.
8. Daisaku Ikeda, *The Human Revolution* (Santa Monica, CA: World Tribune Press, 2004), p. 1724.

19

Karuizawa and the Three Founding Presidents

THE OLYMPICS has its Summer Games and its Winter Games. I had never considered that one city could have hosted competitions for both. But there is such a city: Karuizawa, Japan, has hosted events for both the Summer and Winter Olympics. When curling became an official Olympic sport for the first time at the 1998 Nagano Winter Olympics, that competition took place in Karuizawa.

The 1964 Summer Olympics in Tokyo, Japan, the first Olympic Games to be held in Asia, made Japan's National Stadium, near the Soka Gakkai Headquarters in Shinjuku, its main venue. Few are aware, though, that the equestrian competition for those games took place in Karuizawa. The property that is today the Soka Gakkai's Nagano Training Center was part of the competition grounds, and a monument nearby commemorates the event.

Karuizawa is known today as a summer resort, but during Japan's Edo period (1603–1868) it was a bustling post town along the Nakasendo Highway.[1] With the opening of the Usuishindo

Highway during the Meiji period (1868–1912), this town along the old route grew deserted. But visiting Westerners, who enjoyed the refreshing climate some thirty-two hundred feet above sea level, eventually spurred the area's renewal as a summer resort.

In 1894, Mampei Sato, owner of Karuizawa's Kameya Inn, remodeled the facility to appeal to Western guests and renamed it the Mampei Hotel.

■ ■ ■ ■ ■

President Toda, it seems, was quite fond of Karuizawa, perhaps because its climate resembles that of Hokkaido, where he grew up. In August 1957, the year before he died, he stayed at the Mampei Hotel. Sensing his declining health, Mr. Toda went there to avoid the Tokyo heat. That month—less than one month after my father's release from his two-week detention in connection with the Osaka Incident[2]—President Toda, concerned for my father's health, invited him to Karuizawa along with my mother. My mother, however, was feeling under the weather and did not go. Kazuya Morita accompanied my father to Karuizawa instead. And so it was that my father made his first visit to Karuizawa ten years to the day after his first encounter with President Toda. On August 14, 1947, my father, then only nineteen, had met President Toda at a Soka Gakkai discussion meeting in Kamata, Tokyo. Ten days later, he joined the Soka Gakkai.

During their visit to Karuizawa, President Toda brought my father and Mr. Morita to a place called Onioshidashi on the slope of Mount Asama. Known for its breathtaking and peculiar scenery, it might be described as a garden of fantastically shaped rocks and boulders spread out along the mountainside.

The landscape of Onioshidashi was formed of a lava flow from a 1783 volcanic eruption. Walking through the remnants of that fearsome natural disaster, the three were reminded of the horrible threat posed by nuclear weapons. Their ensuing discussion inspired President Toda's Declaration for the Abolition of Nuclear Weapons, which he made the following month at Mitsuzawa Stadium in Yokohama.

On returning to the hotel, the conversation turned to President Toda's novel, *The Human Revolution*, and on that day, my father resolved strongly to write its sequel.

President Makiguchi had also visited Karuizawa from time to time. From what we can confirm, he went there with President Toda in 1925, 1927 and in August 1928, staying for one week on each occasion. Mr. Makiguchi was then principal of Shirokane Elementary School, and records show that he also led a group of students on a trip to Onioshidashi.

Situated along the Nakasendo Highway that linked Edo[3] and Kyoto, Nagano was exposed to strong cultural influences from both cities and as a result evolved its own rich culture. During the Edo period, what is now Nagano Prefecture was home to as many as 10 percent of the nation's temple schools.[4]

With the initiation of a public elementary school system in the Meiji period, Nagano boasted the nation's highest school attendance rate, establishing itself as a leading prefecture in education. I imagine that is one reason why President Makiguchi, an educator himself, had an interest in going there.

■ ■ ■ ■ ■

By the roadside a few minutes from the Nagano Training Center stands a monument bearing the inscription "Cornerstone of Public Safety." It memorializes those who lost their lives in the 1972 Asama Mountain Lodge Incident, which began when five members of the United Red Army, a radical student group, seized the lodge and took the caretaker's wife hostage. The group barricaded themselves inside the building for ten days as national television news broadcast live images of the perpetrators firing weapons at police. While the hostage was rescued unharmed, two police officers were killed and twenty-six others injured in the melee. It shocked me to learn that one of those arrested in the incident was a high school student around my own age. I reflected deeply on how frightful it is to become misguided in the course of one's education.

Mr. Makiguchi and Mr. Toda had invited young people to Karuizawa and given them opportunities to develop themselves in body and mind. My father, too, on his visits to Karuizawa, has held study and discussion sessions for members of the future and youth divisions, and for SGI members from around the globe, with the aim of fostering able individuals who can contribute to the world of the twenty-first century.

And it was at the Nagano Training Center in Karuizawa that he penned the first manuscript of his novel *The New Human Revolution*. Introducing that work, he shares the following: "What inspired me to write *The New Human Revolution* series as a continuation of *The Human Revolution* was my thought that the extent to which *kosen-rufu* has unfolded since my mentor's passing serves as genuine proof of his greatness. In addition, to transmit my mentor's spirit for eternity, I felt that I must leave a record of the path his disciples, who inherited his legacy, have followed."[5]

On September 8, 1957, President Toda announced his Declaration for the Abolition of Nuclear Weapons, and, as the foremost of his final requests, charged his disciples with disseminating the ideas it contains around the world. On the same day eleven years later (in 1968), my father set forth his proposal for normalizing diplomatic relations between Japan and China. Six years to the day after that, on September 8, 1974, he visited the Soviet Union for the first time. As President Toda's successor, my father has developed and applied the principles expressed in his mentor's Declaration for the Abolition of Nuclear Weapons as a philosophy and movement of peace, culture, education and humanism.

On August 6, 1993, forty-eight years after the first atomic bomb was dropped, he began writing his novel *The New Human Revolution* in Karuizawa.

Published September 25, 2002

Notes

1. The Nakasendo was one of the five main highways controlled by the Shogunate government during Japan's Edo period. It extended 310 miles through Japan's central mountains and included 69 post stations.
See www.nakasendoway.com
2. Osaka Incident— In 1957, after a few Soka Gakkai members campaigning for candidates running for seats in the Upper House were caught violating election laws, authorities in Osaka, in an attempt to suppress the Soka Gakkai, falsely alleged that Daisaku Ikeda had orchestrated the illegal activities. After a four-and-a-half-year court case, Mr. Ikeda was fully acquitted.
3. Edo—the former name of Tokyo.
4. Temple schools —Terakoya, which literally means "temple schools," were private educational institutions, initially set up at Buddhist temples, that taught writing, reading and use of the abacus to the children of Japanese commoners during the Edo period. They enlisted Buddhist priests and samurai as teachers.
5. Daisaku Ikeda, "Introduction" to *The New Human Revolution,* vol. 1 (Santa Monica, CA: World Tribune Press, 1995), pp. ix–x.

The Philosophy of Peace and the Wellspring of Poetic Sentiment

20

Lending Courage to Friends Through Poetry

I BEGAN WRITING this column, "My Path of Youth," for the *Koko Shimpo*, the Soka Gakkai's high school division newspaper, in June 2000. Readers then in their first year of high school will graduate this spring (2003), and many probably have also read my father's essay series "Thoughts on *The New Human Revolution*" carried in the *Seikyo Shimbun*. That series inspired me to write this column.

My father's essay "The City of Cherry Trees" ran in late May 2000. In it, he shares his memories of the flowering cherry trees in his hometown Ota, the planting of one hundred thousand flowering cherry trees to dignify the grounds of the head temple Taiseki-ji,[1] and the naming of the Heian Cherry Tree and Genroku Cherry Tree, the two flowering cherry trees at our home in Shinjuku. After reading it, I decided to write "My Family and the Spring Cherry Blossoms" (the first essay in this volume).

In that essay, I mention the origin of my given name, a story I heard often from my parents while growing up. President Toda proposed the name *Hiromasa*, saying: "Isn't it a fine name? He could become a man of letters." By writing essays, I felt, I might somehow honor President Toda's wish. Through this project, I also wanted to create a journal of my experiences related to the SGI's global movement for peace. Representing my father, I have visited many places around the globe and had the pleasure of meeting many people of wisdom and intellect. It is these experiences I wanted to record and share.

The Japanese word for "essay" (*zuihitsu*) consists of the Chinese characters for "obey" and "brush." It signifies free written expression: literally, to go wherever one's writing brush—or pen—takes one. Composition, I should note, is not my strong suit, and crafting each essay has been a difficult and trying task. Though my writing leaves much to be desired, taking on this challenge nevertheless has enabled me to experience, even to a small degree, how difficult it is to put together words to convey one's intent. I have also gained a new and deeper respect for my father's day-to-day efforts to set down words for the purpose of encouraging others.

■ ■ ■ ■ ■

Since his youth, my father has kept the poetry of Whitman, Dante and Hugo close at hand. Growing up with a weak constitution amid a bleak time of war, he read and recited poetry to spur himself on. This naturally led him to discover joy in composing his own poems. To this day, my father signs his long poems with the pen name Shin'ichi Yamamoto, the name he used to depict himself as a young man in his novel *The Human Revolution*. Perhaps this is because he is expressing through these poems the spirit that permeates the intense struggles he waged as a youth, together with his mentor.

The challenge of writing poetry has been characterized as a

spiritual battle that consumes one's very life. But my father says, "It is my Soka friends who move my heart to create poetry." I can't help thinking that, for him, writing poetry is serving rather to prolong his life.

It is said that the power of imagination that allows one to empathize with others gives rise to the poetic spirit. Throughout the world, we find SGI members who have faced and overcome every imaginable hardship. My father's poems emerge from his heartfelt, compassionate wish to inspire them and give them courage.

The Russian cosmonaut Alexander Serebrov engaged in a dialogue with my father that is being serialized in the monthly magazine *Ushio* starting this month (January 2003). Spaceflight represents the leading edge of science and technology, and might not easily be associated with poetry. But reading the exchanges between these two men, one gains a sense of the thread that links science and the poetic spirit, of the way science and poetry complement and support one another in the search for truth. Mr. Serebrov once said of my father, "President Ikeda extends his concern to our world in the distant future and thinks deeply about the people who will live in that world." And, "Somehow I feel that we are similar people, that we are very much alike."

■ ■ ■ ■ ■

Publication of my father's "Thoughts on *The New Human Revolution*" began August 1, 1998, when he was seventy. In the first essay, he takes stock of his life in ten-year increments:

> To the age of 10: Growing up the son of a humble seaweed harvester.

To the age of 20: Self-awakening and struggling against illnesses.

To the age of 30: Studying and practicing Buddhism, and making earnest efforts to defeat the demons of illness.

To the age of 40: Perfecting my study and practice of Nichiren Daishonin's teachings.

To the age of 50: Making a clear statement in society.

To the age of 60: Completing the foundation for the *kosen-rufu* movement in Japan.

To the age of 70: Establishing the principles of a new humanism.

He also recorded his resolve that by age eighty he would complete the foundation for worldwide *kosen-rufu*.[2]

My father will be seventy-five this January (2003). The last five years have seen the steady development of the foundations for the SGI movement, and the SGI family has grown to include members in 185 countries and territories[3] around the globe. Additionally, in these five years, my father has received more than ninety honorary degrees or titles from universities and institutions of higher learning around the globe (bringing the total number of academic honors to more than 135).[4]

As Nichiren writes, "It is due to the authority and supernatural power of Bodhisattva Universal Worthy that this Lotus Sutra is propagated throughout Jambudvipa."[5] The humanistic principles of Buddhism continue to spread broadly through the power of people of universal wisdom and intellect. Youth of today will inherit the foundations for *kosen-rufu* now being completed.

Last month (December 2002), my father presented to the students of Soka Schools the following poem:

Ascend the path of learning.
A shining castle of glorious victory
Awaits you!

Taking to heart this guiding principle, I pray that 2003 will be a year of glory and great victory for all of you.

Published January 1, 2003

Notes

1. Beginning in 1992, Nikken ordered that 218 cherry trees at Taiseki-ji be cut down. These cherry trees were donated by the Soka Gakkai during the construction of the temple, symbolizing the joy and sincere faith of millions of practitioners.
2. "Thoughts on *The New Human Revolution*" (later "Light of the Century of Humanity) began publication on August 1, 1998, in the Soka Gakkai's daily newspaper, *Seikyo Shimbun*. See also January 23, 1998, *World Tribune*, p. 4.
3. As of August 24, 2008, the SGI's movement for peace, culture and education has spread to 192 countries and territories around the world.
4. As of July 2008, there have been more than 240 academic titles conferred upon SGI President Daisaku Ikeda from institutions of higher learning throughout the world.
5. *The Record of the Orally Transmitted Teachings* (Tokyo: Soka Gakkai, 2004), p. 190.

21

The Significance of the "Gandhi, King, Ikeda" Exhibition

LAST MONTH (September 2002), the exhibition "Gandhi, King, Ikeda—A Legacy of Building Peace" went on display at Soka University in Japan. Among those attending the opening ceremonies on September 12 were Dr. Lawrence Edward Carter Sr.—dean of the Martin Luther King Jr. International Chapel and the person who conceived of and proposed the exhibition—and Dr. Aftab Seta, the Indian Ambassador to Japan. Sponsored by the Morehouse College Martin Luther King Jr. International Chapel, the exhibition first opened at Morehouse College in Atlanta, Georgia, in April last year (2001). Before coming to Japan, it had toured to more than twenty cities throughout the United States.

To be honest, when I first heard of Dr. Carter's proposal of an exhibition featuring Mahatma Gandhi, India's father of independence, Dr. Martin Luther King Jr., leader of the non-violent civil rights movement in the United States, and SGI President Ikeda, I was quite surprised that my father was included along with such world-renowned figures. But there is a strong thread that links Soka Gakkai presidents Makiguchi and Toda to Mahatma Gandhi and Dr. King. That is the spirit of being willing to sacrifice oneself in order to launch a popular movement grounded in nonviolence.

Dr. Carter offered me the following: "Gandhi and King have gradually been deified by the generations that followed them. I do not believe that is what either of them desired. I am convinced that Daisaku Ikeda is a living example of continually advancing toward the same goals as those two drum majors for social justice. I want to include the name *Ikeda* in this project so that the spirit of both Mahatma Gandhi and Dr. King can be kept alive in the present and in the future. Introducing the life of SGI President Ikeda in this exhibition will allow the American people to understand correctly the Buddhist ideal of humanism as a grassroots movement inherited from presidents Makiguchi and Toda, as well as the ideal of world peace that the SGI is striving to attain. These ideals strongly resonate with, and can support a deeper understanding of, the ideals of Mahatma Gandhi and Dr. King." From the bottom of my heart, I thank Dr. Carter and the people of Morehouse College for their deep understanding of the SGI's activities to promote peace based on Buddhist values.

■ ■ ■ ■ ■

Atlanta, Georgia, where Morehouse College is located, is known worldwide as the city that hosted the 1996 Summer Olympics and as the birthplace of such global corporate giants as Coca-Cola and the CNN news network. During the American Civil War, Atlanta was devastated by Union troops, a history that became the backdrop for Margaret Mitchell's famous novel,

Gone With the Wind. Morehouse, founded just after the American Civil War in 1867, is a private, historically black liberal arts college for men. It is the alma mater of Dr. Martin Luther King Jr., whose father and grandfather were also Morehouse graduates as is his eldest son. Nelson Mandela, the South African champion of civil rights, visited the United States in 1990, following his release after twenty-seven years of imprisonment. During that trip, Mr. Mandela received invitations to speak from numerous colleges and universities and from five American cities, but spoke at only one American college—Morehouse College. There he received honorary doctoral degrees from thirty-seven colleges and universities in the Martin Luther King Jr. International Chapel.[1] Mr. Mandela's choosing Morehouse points to the stature and important role of this college.

■ ■ ■ ■ ■

Gandhi, King and Ikeda are three men who never met. Dr. King was a student at Morehouse College from 1944 to 1948 when Mr. Gandhi was assassinated at age seventy-eight. At a memorial service held for Mahatma Gandhi on the Morehouse campus, Dr. King's assigned seat was in the front row, directly in front of the podium. Morehouse President Benjamin E. Mays delivered the tribute.[2] Ten years later, Dr. King visited India to study Gandhi's nonviolent philosophy and tactics. Upon his return to the United States, he wrote the following in a letter to Dr. G. Ramachandran, who had arranged his visit: "As a result of my visit to India, I believe that my understanding of nonviolence is greater and my commitment deeper. I have tried to get this message over America since I have returned to the country."[3]

My father visited the Gandhi Memorial Museum in India

in 1992, traced Gandhi's last footsteps,[4] and delivered a lecture in his memory. In that lecture, he quoted Gandhi's observation that "good travels at a snail's pace"[5] and continued: "Mr. Gandhi's idea of reform is clearly a gradual change, not a radical societal revolution. I believe that his sense of reality and sense of order, in many respects, resonates with the Buddhist ideal of the Middle Way."

Mahatma Gandhi was an Indian of the Hindu faith, Dr. King was an African-American Christian, and my father is a Japanese Buddhist. The three men share no common country, culture or religion, but all have upheld lofty ideals and endeavored to realize those ideals by promoting nonviolence and dialogue. It is the purpose of this exhibition, I believe, to highlight just that.

Gandhi won independence for his native India through the consistent application of non-violent resistance against the might of the British Empire. King succeeded in abolishing legalized discrimination in the United States by fighting against the racial prejudice so deeply entrenched in American society. But the global society that these two men envisioned has yet to be realized, as violence and prejudice continue unchecked in many parts of the world. This exhibition conveys the purpose of the SGI and its activities—to become a bastion for realizing the peaceful world that Gandhi and King imagined.

Gandhi said, "True nonviolence is an impossibility without the possession of unadulterated fearlessness."[6] Even if one's opponents have authority and weapons—if they are in the wrong, to firmly stand one's ground for what is right is the essence of nonviolence.

I believe that this ideology of Gandhi has its roots in Buddhism. In fact, it seems that Gandhi studied Buddhism. Nichiren teaches, "One day of life is more valuable than all the treasures of the major world system."⁷

Buddhism makes the absolute sanctity of life its foundation. And the principles of nonviolence live on today in the philosophy and work of the Soka Gakkai's three founding presidents, who thoroughly put the principles of Buddhism into practice.

Our young members are the successors to this great legacy. Always bearing this in mind as you go about your daily activities, I believe, will empower you to make a significant personal contribution to the building of peace.

Published October 9, 2002.

Notes

1. The presidents of all thirty-seven colleges and universities attended the ceremony.
2. It should be noted that Morehouse College President Benjamin E. Mays' homage to Mahatma Gandhi was based on the time that he had spent personally with Gandhi interviewing him at his ashram in 1936. President Mays helped introduce the ideas of Mahatma Gandhi to Martin Luther King Jr.
3. Martin Luther King Jr., *The Papers of Martin Luther King Jr.: Volume VI: Advocate of the Social Gospel, September 1948–March 1963* (Berkeley and Los Angeles, CA: University of California Press, 2007), pp. 211–12.
4. Gandhi's last footsteps, which are marked in cement on the path where he was walking at the time he was assassinated, at the Gandhi Memorial Museum in India.
5. M.K. Gandhi, *Hind Swaraj and Other Writings*, ed. Anthony J. Parel, (Cambridge, MA: Cambridge University Press, 1997), p. 47.
6. M.K. Gandhi, *Harijan*, July 15, 1939; M.K. Gandhi, *All Men Are Brothers*, (London: Continuum International Publishing Group, 1980), p. 92.
7. Major world system—One of the world systems described in ancient Indian cosmology and mentioned in the Lotus Sutra. One major world system is said to comprise one billion worlds. The quote mentioned here is from *The Writings of Nichiren Daishonin*, vol. 1, p. 955.

22

The Legacy of the Pauling Family

THIS YEAR'S (2002) Nobel Prizes seem to have attracted more attention here in Japan than those of recent years. For the first time, two Japanese citizens have won in the same year, and for the third straight year, a Japanese has won the Nobel Prize in Chemistry. Another reason for so much attention may be the disparity in the winners' backgrounds: the prize winner in physics is an emeritus professor at the University of Tokyo in his seventies, while the winner in chemistry is a salaried researcher for a major company in his forties.

The level of excitement surrounding the Nobel Prizes does not seem to be as high in Europe or the United States as it is in Japan. Perhaps because Americans have won about 40 percent of all Nobel Prizes, the announcement of the prizewinners in the United States attracts only light news coverage.

But even amid such relative indifference, there is someone widely recognized and respected in America as the only person to have won two unshared Nobel Prizes. That is Dr. Linus Pauling, winner of the Nobel Prize in Chemistry and the Nobel Peace Prize, which honor his work in two completely different fields. Dr. Pauling, it is said, was even considered for a third Nobel Prize.

Soka University in Japan is now (in November 2002) hosting an exhibition celebrating the life of Dr. Pauling called "Linus Pauling and the Twentieth Century." That exhibition has been touring Japan since April, appearing already in Hiroshima, Kobe, Nagasaki and Yokohama.

■ ■ ■ ■ ■

Born in 1901, Dr. Pauling was a contemporary of second Soka Gakkai president Josei Toda, who was born in 1900. Pauling became interested in chemistry in his early teens. When Linus Pauling was only nine, his father died of an illness. Beset financially, his mother ran a boarding house to provide income to support herself and her three children. She wanted Linus to find work, as well. But because his grades in school were so good, he entered the Oregon Agricultural College (later Oregon State University) at sixteen on the advice of a friend.

While attending college, Linus worked part time to finance his education and to send money home. Even so, his mother needed additional financial help. To provide for her further, he took a year off from his studies between his junior and senior years to work full time.

Dr. Pauling's mother died in 1926, when he was twenty-five. Just five years later, in 1931, he gained recognition as a scientist, when he received the American Chemical Society Award in Pure Chemistry (the Langmuir Prize) for meritorious work by a young chemist. Recalling that time in later years, he spoke regretfully of his mother not having lived to see him receive the award.

Dr. Pauling won the Nobel Prize in Chemistry in 1954, the same year Ernest Hemingway won the prize for literature. Though happy at the news, Dr. Pauling said: "I was pleased but not really surprised because rumor of its coming to me had been abroad for some time. . . . The Nobel Prize was given to me for doing work I enjoyed."[1] Nonetheless, winning the Nobel Peace Prize eight years later took him completely by surprise. At the time, he said that having received it made working for peace respectable.[2]

■ ■ ■ ■ ■

My father met Dr. Pauling for the first time in February 1987, at the Soka University campus in Calabasas. Dr. Pauling was then approaching eighty-six. Just five years earlier, he had lost his beloved wife, his lifelong partner.

My father and Dr. Pauling met again in February 1990 at the Los Angeles campus. A collection of their dialogues was published in Japanese in the fall of that year, and then in English in 1992 as *A Lifelong Quest for Peace*. For Dr. Pauling, who died two years later, these dialogues may well have served as a final opportunity to recount his life and accomplishments. I heard that he kept copies of the book stacked on his desk and handed them out with a smile to everyone who visited him.

The following observation by his son, Dr. Linus Pauling Jr., impressed me: "My father was not very good at connecting with people or their hearts and minds. But with President Ikeda, he could share his thoughts and feelings in a friendly manner. I believe he could do so because Mr. Ikeda unlocked his emotions and opened up his heart."[3]

Dr. Pauling and my father met again at a San Francisco hotel in 1993, the year before his death. During this last meeting, my father proposed the idea of a Pauling exhibition. Dr. Pauling gave his consent and asked my father to discuss details with his eldest son, Dr. Linus Pauling Jr.,[4] who lived in Hawaii. Five years later, in September 1998, the "Linus Pauling and the Twentieth Century" exhibition opened in San Francisco. Several prominent scientists, including five Nobel laureates, attended the opening ceremony, as did Dr. Pauling's younger sister, who was still very spry despite being more than ninety, and several of Dr. Pauling's acquaintances. US Vice President Al Gore sent a congratulatory message. I also attended the event.

Addressing the attendees, Dr. Pauling Jr. said: "Unfortunately, I did not inherit all of my father's talents. But I believe that there are some people in attendance today who will carry on my father's talents and achievements."[5] As he spoke about his father, I sensed his heartfelt delight at the exhibition's opening.

One section of the exhibition in particular caught my eye: a photo of the White House flanked on each side by photos of Dr. and Mrs. Pauling. One photo showed the couple dancing in formal wear, and in the other, they held up placards at a demonstration against atmospheric nuclear testing. Actually, these two pictures were taken on the same day in April 1962—one at a dinner party hosted by President John F. Kennedy honoring Nobel Prize recipients, and the other at a demonstration that encircled the White House. Dr. and Mrs. Pauling had been invited to both events. During the day, they marched in protest outside the White House, and at night, they attended the President's dinner party inside the White House. This episode is emblematic of the couple's character and beliefs.

That fall, Dr. Pauling was awarded the Nobel Prize for Peace. On receiving that honor, he commented: "Since 1923, I have had always at my side my wife, Ava Helen Pauling. In the fight for peace and against oppression, she has been my constant and courageous companion and co-worker."[6] Dr. Pauling further commented that being presented with this award for his work was really an indirect recognition of his wife's success.

The Linus Pauling exhibition celebrates the shared triumph of a husband and wife devoted to advancing peace and science. Further, with their son carrying on their efforts, the exhibition represents the triumph of a family united in their commitment to a mission. Linus Pauling Jr., who turned seventy-seven in 2002, attended all of the exhibition's showings in five cities in Japan and graciously spoke at each.

■ ■ ■ ■ ■

The first event at the opening ceremonies for Soka University of America in May 2001 was the dedication of the Linus and Ava Helen Pauling Hall, a classroom building on campus. Dr. Pauling Jr., who attended the event, expressed his expectation that SUA produce a steady stream of able individuals, including future Nobel laureates. A bust of Dr. Pauling on display at the exhibition now stands at the Linus and Ava Helen Pauling Hall at SUA, and a replica of the same figure is on display at the Tokyo Soka High School.

In July next year (2003), students from that school will

represent Japan in the International Chemistry Olympiad in Athens. The Soka students scheduled to compete in the Olympiad attended the opening ceremony of the "Linus Pauling and the Twentieth Century" exhibition at Soka University, each of them exchanging a firm handshake with Dr. Pauling Jr. Observing this, I sensed deeply that the Pauling exhibition is not simply about chronicling past achievements; rather, it is aimed at developing talented individuals who will shoulder the challenges of the twenty-first century.

Published November 13, 2002

NOTES

1. Linus Pauling and Daisaku Ikeda, *A Lifelong Quest for Peace: A Dialogue* (Boston: Jones and Bartlett Publishers, 1992), p. 15.
2. *A Lifelong Quest for Peace: A Dialogue*, p. 15.
3. Translated from Japanese.
4. Linus Pauling Jr., MD, graduated from Harvard Medical School in 1952.
5. Translated from Japanese.
6. From the Oregon State University Libraries, Special Collections http://osulibrary.oregonstate.edu/specialcollections/coll/pauling/peace/notes/1963s.-1-ts-02.html

23

Thoughts on Mount Fuji
As Seen From Space

In its 2003 New Year's Day issue, the *Seikyo Shimbun* began serializing volume 14 of *The New Human Revolution*. The first chapter of that volume, "Wisdom and Courage," begins describing events that took place in May 1969.

The radical student movement in Japan was then at its peak, and the fervor of student uprisings was spreading throughout the country. That was the year I entered high school. Since the school I attended was on the same grounds as a university campus, I got an up-close sense of the unrest. Sometimes a barricade of chairs and desks blocked the main entrance, and we had to find another way into the school.

When I entered the university just three years later, not a trace of student discord remained. The campus was now peaceful and calm, and it became clear to me just how empty and futile that kind of "revolutionary movement" can be.

That year (1969), we also witnessed the success of the first manned moon landing—America's Apollo 11. Touching down on July 21 at just past five in the morning, Japan time, Mission

Commander Neil Armstrong took his first step onto the lunar surface at about noon. I remember sitting with our eyes glued to the black-and-white TV screen, watching the images broadcast live from the moon. Commander Armstrong's first words as he set foot on the moon's surface impressed me deeply: "That's one small step for a man, one giant leap for mankind." The US space project Apollo, developed in the 1960s, had been designed to put people on the moon and bring them back safely to Earth.

In the 1970s, the United States and the Soviet Union embarked on a joint space venture called the Apollo-Soyuz Test Project, testing the compatibility of rendezvous and docking systems to use between American and Soviet spacecraft.

The first Space Shuttle was launched in the 1980s, and the Space Shuttle program continues today. The name *Space Shuttle* seems very fitting for a spacecraft that can repeatedly carry people into space and back again. Five shuttles have been built in all, flying more than one hundred space missions since the first launch of the shuttle *Columbia* in 1981. During this time, four Japanese astronauts have flown on seven shuttle missions.[1]

I have heard that the final episode of NHK's [Japan's national broadcasting corporation] current television drama series *Manten* will show the heroine [Manten Hidaka, played by Mao Miyaji] boarding a space shuttle and launching into orbit. This perhaps indicates how commonplace the idea of spaceflight has become.

The January (2003) launch of the space shuttle *Columbia* drew little attention in Japan. I was not even aware of the flight until I saw, in the newspaper, photos taken from space of Mount Fuji, snow clearly visible blanketing the top half of the mountain. On January 31, astronaut Laurel Clark aboard *Columbia* wrote this e-mail to her family: "Mount Fuji looks like a small bump from up here, but it does stand out as a very distinct landmark."²

Sadly, the very next day (February 1), after completing its sixteen-day journey, *Columbia* disintegrated upon reentering the earth's atmosphere, taking with it the lives of all seven crewmembers. It was the first such tragedy since the *Challenger* disaster in 1986, seventeen years earlier. Prior to launch, the *Challenger* mission had received great attention because the crew included the first private citizen, a female high school teacher. Tragically, that shuttle exploded immediately after launch, sacrificing the entire crew.

Russian cosmonaut Dr. Alexander Serebrov, in his dialogues with my father published in the monthly magazine *Ushio*, states that on three occasions he thought he would die in space and had mentally prepared himself for death. "We [astronauts and cosmonauts] have the responsibility to use space exploration to benefit humanity; we owe it to those pioneers of spaceflight who sacrificed their precious lives for the advancement of humankind."

■ ■ ■ ■ ■

The photos of Mount Fuji seen from space were taken on January 26 (2003). On this day, which also happened to be the anniversary of the SGI's founding, my father met with Dr. Serebrov at the offices of the *Seikyo Shimbun* and said to him: "My late mentor (Josei Toda) was a proponent of 'global citizenship.' Seen from space, the Earth must really seem like one single home. All races of people are citizens of the earth. Never has there been a time when this universal perspective was more necessary than it is today." President Toda first put forth his vision of global citizenship in 1952, during that year's Soka Gakkai youth division study course. At that time, the United States and the Soviet Union were in the midst of the Cold War; the first manmade satellite had not yet been launched, let alone a manned spacecraft. At this point in history, President Toda appealed to young people with his concept of global citizenship—a universal perspective transcending national and ideological differences. The SGI's activities aim at carrying on this ideal and working to make it a reality.

The SGI was founded on January 26, 1975, and my father became its president. On January 26 every year since 1983, he has presented a peace proposal to the United Nations. This year (2003), he delivered his twenty-first annual peace proposal, in which he states: "We cannot remain passive in the face of these severe realities. Rather, we should open ourselves to the limitless power, the unstoppable dynamic of change that is created when awakened people unite and act together. It is in proving this truth that humanity in the twenty-first century can fulfill its mission."[3] Indeed, the world today seems veiled in a dark cloud of gloom, and this underscores our great mission as SGI members to be the united bearers of a humanistic philosophy.

■ ■ ■ ■ ■

My father first announced the three mottoes of Soka University, which it adopted as its founding principles, in May 1969—two years before the school opened. That was at the height of the unrest striking university campuses around the country. I believe it inspired him to write the motto "Be a fortress for the peace of humankind." He wanted Soka University to be like a fortress, to protect their right to a peaceful and happy existence.

Continuing his dialogue with Dr. Serebrov, my father said, "In the coming era, a viewpoint that calls for us to 'think universally and act globally' will be of vital importance." The unified efforts of people who subscribe to this viewpoint of universal citizenship can transform the times. I believe it is up to Soka University to embrace and protect such people, to be a fortress in which they can create the solidarity of peace.

Published February 26, 2003

Notes

1. As of February 26, 2003, when this essay was published.
2. February 2, 2003, Associated Press.
3. Daisaku Ikeda, "A Global Ethic of Coexistence: Toward a 'Life-Sized' Paradigm for Our Age" (Santa Monica, CA: April 2003 *Living Buddhism*), p. 23.

24

Bold As Mount Fuji

As a native of Tokyo, I've been accustomed since childhood to the sight of Mount Fuji in the distance. When I was in elementary school, my family lived in Tokyo's Ota Ward, and I enjoyed views of the mountain from my maternal grandparents' home in Yaguchi, as well as from along the banks of the nearby Tama River, where I often went to play.

After I entered junior high school, we moved to Shinjuku Ward in Tokyo, where my parents have lived since. From the *Seikyo Shimbun* publishing offices near our house, I could get a clear look at Mount Fuji, though today taller buildings block the view.

As I rode the train to and from high school, I sometimes caught glimpses of Mount Fuji while crossing the bridge spanning the Tama River. In those days, the air in Tokyo was very polluted—much more than now. To see Mount Fuji on a rare clear day refreshed our spirits.

When it came to choosing the location for the Soka Schools campus in Tokyo, one condition my father set was that the site would have a good view of Mount Fuji.

Thirty-five years ago (in 1968), I attended the first entrance ceremony for Soka Schools along with my parents and my younger brother Takahiro. I was then in my third year of junior high school,[1] and Takahiro was in the fourth grade of elementary school. I think it's interesting that, having attended this first ceremony together, my brother and I eventually both ended up working for Soka Schools.

On that day, ceremonies were held to formally open Glory Bridge (Eikobashi), which spans the Tama River Aqueduct running alongside the campus.

I clearly remember the scene from atop the bridge, of Mount Fuji soaring beyond the mottled groves of trees on Musashino plain. No matter how my surroundings change, I always feel a fond nostalgia when I see Mount Fuji in the distance.

That autumn, a dormitory song titled "Kusaki wa moyuru" [The grass and trees flourish] was composed for Soka Schools. A dorm resident from Osaka wrote the lyrics up through the fourth verse, and my father contributed the fifth verse:

> *We can see Mount Fuji from Musashino*
> *Where pure streams flow.*
> *For what purpose*
> *Do we young phoenixes work for peace?*
> *To open a path for wonderful friends,*
> *You and I, together,*
> *Let us take flight into the future.*

Today it has become the school song, sung not only by the students but by people throughout Japan and around the world.

The Soka University student song, too, evokes an image of Mount Fuji:

Beyond the broad blue mountains,
Stands Mount Fuji!
For you who pursue bold ideals,
The matchless peak soars,
Dyed in pure white.

From this we can sense the hope that those who study in these halls watched over by Mount Fuji will develop confidence and conviction as firm and immovable as the mountain itself.

■ ■ ■ ■ ■

This year (2003), in a long poem published on February 1 (titled "The Splendid Stage of Greater Tokyo—Capital of *Kosen-rufu*"), my father wrote:

Tokugawa Ieyasu[2]
always made it his rule
to choose for his castle
a site with a view of Mount Fuji.

In that place,
where one could
gaze out at the Kanto plain,
and see in the distance
the graceful form of Mount Fuji,
there Ieyasu would make his headquarters,
and there build his castle,
to unite all under heaven.

Tokugawa Ieyasu rose to the position of "Great Shogun" and founded the Edo Shogunate government in February 1603. The poem continues,

> And in that land, he conceived his dream, his resolve,
> to take up command and build a prosperous realm
> that would thrive for ten thousand years.

In accord with Ieyasu's wishes, the era of peace and prosperity he founded lasted more than two hundred years.

This year, we recognize the four-hundredth anniversary of the founding of the Edo Shogunate. It is also the hundredth anniversary of the publication of first Soka Gakkai president Makiguchi's book *A Geography of Human Life*. At the time he wrote it, Japan was moving from its involvement in the first Sino-Japanese War into the Russo-Japanese War, and the world at large was heading quickly toward the outbreak of World War I. In the midst of that age of conflict, President Makiguchi published this book, which had as its main theme the relationship between the environment and the way people live. Transcending awareness based on race or nationality, he aimed to awaken people to their status as world citizens. In *A Geography of Human Life*, Mr. Makiguchi writes, "Mountains ease the human spirit and illuminate the human heart," and "How much has Mount Fuji contributed to the Japanese people's sense of solemnity."

Mount Fuji not only boasts the highest elevation in Japan, but, because the hills and mountains surrounding it are relatively low, it conveys in its towering solitude a particular sense of presence and beauty. Throughout Japan, some three hundred mountains are known as the "Fuji" of this place or that region.

From this, we can see how dearly the people of Japan regard the mountain.

Fuji's simple form displays any number of expressions, according to the season, the weather and the time of day. My father has taken many photos of Mount Fuji from locations such as Shizuoka Prefecture, Yamanashi Prefecture and Soka University in Hachioji, Tokyo, as well as from the air. One of these photos he gave as a present to former Soviet President Mikhail Gorbachev.

That was in May 1994, about two-and-a-half years after the Soviet Union had dissolved and Mr. Gorbachev stepped down as president, and a little more than a year after he and his wife, Raisa, had paid their first visit to Soka University in Japan.

The 1994 meeting, which I also attended, took place in the office of Mr. Gorbachev's foundation in Moscow. My father said: "You have been living your life with the serenity of Mount Fuji, with the boldness of Mount Fuji. This picture reminds me of that."

Mr. Gorbachev seemed delighted, and replied: "I am greatly inspired by this picture. I shall display it on my office wall where I can see it every day."

Today it still hangs in a special room in the newly built headquarters of Mr. Gorbachev's foundation.

■ ■ ■ ■ ■

February 23 is designated "Mount Fuji Day" (because the numbers 2-2-3 can be pronounced "fu-ji-san" in Japanese, meaning "Mount Fuji"). On that date this year, a ceremony to bestow upon my father an honorary doctorate from the National University of Piura in Peru was conducted at the Central Tower of

Soka University. It was my father's one hundred fortieth such honor from a world institution of higher learning.

In Eiji Yoshikawa's novel *Miyamoto Musashi*, we find this passage: "Rather than worrying about your future, thinking, 'Perhaps I should become this. Perhaps I should become that,' first be still and build a self that is as solid and unmoving as Mount Fuji. Never court the favor of people in society. If you become someone who is looked up to by others, then the world will naturally accord you the value you merit."[3]

My father first heard this passage from his homeroom teacher as a fifth-grade student. He has never since forgotten it and often shares it with young people. Please understand that our day-to-day efforts in study and in faith are to enable us to forge a character as solid and unmovable as Mount Fuji.

Published March 12, 2003

Notes

1. The corresponding grade in the United States is ninth grade.
2. Tokugawa Ieyasu (1543–1616) was a military leader and statesman, founder and first shogun of the Tokugawa Shogunate of Japan, which ruled from 1600 until the Meiji Restoration in 1868. Ieyasu organized new laws to regulate the court and the military clans, and laid the foundations for more than 250 years of peace under Tokugawa rule during the Edo period (1600–1867), which is also known as the beginning of the early modern period of Japanese history.
3. Eiji Yoshikawa, *Miyamoto Musashi* (Tokyo: Rokko Shuppan-bu, 1965), vol. 5, p. 8.

25

The Hakone Long-Distance Relay

A NUMBER of sports events take place in Japan over the New Year's holiday. These include the National High School Soccer Tournament, in which Soka High School participated for the first time in 1981, twenty-two years ago, and the National High School Rugby Tournament. The latter was a source of disappointment for Kansai Soka High School this year (2003), as its chance to participate slipped away when it lost the lottery that decides which schools will compete.

But the event that attracted the most attention this year may have been the seventy-ninth annual Tokyo-Hakone college relay (Hakone Ekiden). The two-day race takes place January 2 and 3. Ten-member college relay teams run a course from Tokyo to the shore of Lake Ashi at the mountain resort town of Hakone and back—a total distance of more than one hundred twenty miles. In a typical track-and-field relay, each runner carries and passes on a baton to the next runner on the team. But in *ekiden* races, marathon relays that originated in Japan, the runners wear a sash, which they pass on to the next runner. And running each leg (averaging about twelve miles) of this long-distance race wearing a sash is certainly easier than doing so holding a baton.

I was a sprinter on my high school track team and never competed in an *ekiden*, but I love watching them and look forward to the Hakone race every year.

Traditionally, fifteen teams have competed in the Hakone relay. This year (2003), though, the field was expanded to twenty teams. Of the twenty, one was an all-star team—a first in the race's history.

For a team to make it to the Hakone relay, it must either be seeded by placing high (among the top ten) in the previous year's race or qualify through a preliminary race. Qualification in the preliminary is based on each ten-member team's aggregate time, a measure of its overall performance. Of the dozens of schools that compete in the preliminary, the six top-performing teams qualify automatically for the Hakone relay. The remaining slots are filled by teams selected from among the preliminary competitors according to their performance in the previous year's Kanto region[1] intercollegiate competitions. Soka University has yet to break through this barrier and qualify a team for the Hakone race.

The purpose of the all-star team is to give top college runners from schools whose teams have not qualified a chance to run in the Hakone relay. These runners compete wearing their school track uniform. This year (2003), two runners from Soka University were selected for the all-star team.[2] Tenma Nozaki, a senior, ended up competing and really gave his all.

My high school (Keio Gijuku High) was in Yokohama, Kanagawa Prefecture. I ran in track meets at such venues as Yokohama's Mitsuzawa Stadium and the sports stadium in Fujisawa. For the first meet of my freshman year, I remember leaving my house in Shinano-machi, Tokyo, very early in the morning and arriving at Mitsuzawa Stadium before anyone else to save seats for my team.

My ability as a short-distance runner qualified me only for opening prefecture-level tournaments at best. But in the relay event, our team was among the strongest, advancing to the finals every year. In long-distance events, Aihara High School was the Kanagawa Prefecture powerhouse that stood head and shoulders above the rest. I remember the strong impression I had of the Aihara runners, who always led in the prefecture meets. And when Aihara High won the National Inter-High School Competition and National High School Relay, as a fellow runner from the same prefecture, I felt happy for them.

In this year's Hakone event, a runner from Juntendo University made big news when he passed fifteen runners, setting a new record. The previous record had been set in 1974 in the fiftieth Hakone race, when Makoto Hattori of Tokyo University of Agriculture passed twelve runners. Hattori had been a member of the Aihara High School track team and had always led in the Kanagawa Prefectural high school tournaments.

One of Hattori's teammates at Aihara back then was Makoto Sato, who today coaches the Soka University track team. Coach Sato had also gone on to attend Tokyo University of Agriculture and ran with Hattori in the fiftieth Hakone relay. That year, Tokyo University of Agriculture for the first time won the first half of the race (from Tokyo to Hakone). When Mr. Sato was appointed Soka University track coach in 1996, I was pleasantly surprised. It brought back to me those high school track memories, and I knew our team was in good hands.

And so it came to be that Coach Sato this year sent his first runners from Soka University to the Hakone relay. Soka

University competitor Nozaki ran the fourth leg of the race, from Hiratsuka to Odawara. Coincidentally, it was the same leg that Coach Sato ran in 1974.

When I taught at Kansai Soka High School, I also served as an advisor to the track team. I remember taking the team regularly to compete at venues such as Osaka Nagai Stadium and Banpaku Stadium. At the time, I never dreamed that our team would qualify for national competitions. But now, not only our track team, but our baseball, rugby and kendo teams compete at the national level.

I look forward to the day when Soka University will send a team to the Hakone Ekiden relay. As I watched this year's race, I envisioned a ten-member Soka team, their uniforms decorated with the three colors of the Soka Schools, giving it their all.

To congratulate Soka University on sending its first runners to the Hakone relay, my father wrote this poem:

Soka University's envoys
made a dignified showing
in the Hakone Ekiden,
our historic treasure!

Published January 22, 2003

Notes

1. The Kanto region of Honshu, the largest island of Japan, encompasses seven prefectures, which overlap the greater Tokyo area: Gunma, Tochigi, Ibaraki, Saitama, Tokyo, Chiba and Kanagawa.
2. For the Hakone relay all-star team, of the two runners selected from each university, one was chosen to compete and the other, a standby.

26

To My Friends in Taiwan—
Winter Always Turns to Spring

TOKUGAWA IEYASU[1] founded the Edo Shogunate in 1603, on the twelfth day of the second month, by the lunar calendar of the time. On the modern solar calendar, that would correspond to March 24, and so March 24 this year (2003) marked the four-hundredth anniversary of the Edo Shogunate.

Also on that day, a ceremony was held to award honorary doctorates to my father and mother from the Chinese Culture University in Taiwan. At the Central Tower of Soka University, CCU Board of Regents Chairman Chang Jen-hu and his wife, along with CCU President Lin Tsai-mei, presented my father with an honorary doctorate in philosophy and my mother with an honorary doctorate in law. It was my father's first honorary degree from a university in Taiwan, and my mother's third such degree overall, following honorary doctorates from the University of Flores in Argentina and Fujian Normal University in China.

Chinese Culture University was founded in March 1962 by Chairman Chang's father, Dr. Chang Chi-yun. When CCU first opened, its student body numbered a mere eighty. Today it boasts the largest number of departments (eleven) of any university in Taiwan and a student body of more than twenty thousand.

While CCU is nearly ten years Soka University's senior, a number of interesting facts connect the two schools: Chairman Chang and my father (the founder of Soka University) are of the same generation, and CCU's founder, Dr. Chang, was born in 1901, which would make him a contemporary of President Toda. Dr. Chang was a prominent geographer and historian who wrote a book titled *A Geography of Human Life*—coincidentally, the very same title as a book by President Makiguchi, the originator of Soka education. Dr. Chang is also said to have conducted research on Dr. Arnold Toynbee, whom he held in high regard. And I understand that his son, Chairman Chang, has been quite fond of *Choose Life*, the collection of dialogues between Dr. Toynbee and my father, since even before he met my father in 1994.

President Lin studied at Kinki University in Osaka, Japan, as an exchange student and speaks exceptionally fluent Japanese. She told me that when she was in elementary school, one of her teachers, a Japanese woman, had been very kind to her, and that experience led her to take an interest in learning Japanese.

Taiwan is an island slightly smaller than Kyushu (Japan's southernmost and third-largest main island), and its rich natural landscape moved Portuguese sailors to name it *Isla Formosa*, or, "Beautiful Island." And yet, its history is one of great turbulence. For fifty years, from the First Sino-Japanese War (August 1, 1894–April 17, 1895) through World War II, Taiwan was ruled by Japan, and many Japanese migrated there during that period. After World War II, it was determined that the island would be returned to China. But that was just as the Chinese Civil War erupted between Mao Tse-tung's Communist Party forces and the Nationalist Party forces of Chiang Kai-shek. The Communist Party ultimately gained control of the mainland, and in 1949, established the People's Republic of China in Beijing. Nationalist Party troops, officials and supporters fled to Taiwan, and there established the Republic of China, the name its government retains today.

The Soka Gakkai was first established in Taiwan in August 1962, with the launch of its Taipei Chapter. Chu Wan Lee, the first chapter leader, later became the general director of Soka Gakkai Taiwan. During World War II, Mr. Chu had studied at Waseda University in Japan. He later joined the Soka Gakkai after being encouraged to do so by a Japanese friend. At that time, personal freedom of religion was recognized in Taiwan, but government permission was required to conduct religious activities as a group. Anti-Japanese sentiment still ran strong in those days, and the government declined to grant the Japan-born Soka Gakkai recognition.

On January 27, 1963, my father was in Hong Kong after completing a series of activities in Southeast Asia. When his direct flight home to Tokyo was cancelled, he had to board a flight that stopped over in Taipei, Taiwan's capital. This turn of events had been unexpected, but when my father arrived at Taipei's Songshan Airport, Chapter Leader Chu and about fifty Soka Gakkai members were there to greet him. Using the limited time he had while his plane refueled, he earnestly encouraged the members, telling them: "No matter what happens, no matter how hard things become, for the well-being of the Taiwanese people, I hope that you will not allow the flame of Nichiren Daishonin's Buddhism to be extinguished. True victory will be apparent thirty or forty years down the line. You will definitely triumph in the end. . . . Winter never fails to turn to spring. . . . Times change. And you can change things through your prayers."[2]

In April, only two months after that dramatic encounter, the Soka Gakkai Taipei Chapter received from the government an order to disband. For the Taiwanese members, the "winter" my father had spoken of suddenly arrived. Nevertheless, bolstered by the encouragement he had given them at Songshan Airport, they used this opportunity to strengthen their faith and deepen their conviction, devoting themselves to cultural activities in order to gain the trust of their society.

Eventually, democratization came to Taiwan, and laws restricting religion became less stringent. Finally, in 1990, the Soka Gakkai became an officially registered organization in Taiwan. Furthermore, through its cultural activities and the powerful solidarity its members had cultivated over the years, the Soka Gakkai Taiwan has made significant contributions to Taiwanese society. For ten consecutive years since 1992, the Taiwan Ministry of the Interior has recognized it as an "excellent community organization."[3] Additionally, in April 2002, the Ministry of the Interior conferred on my father its "Award of the Highest Order," which I accepted on his behalf. The award honored my father for "proactively contributing to cultural and educational exchange between Japan and Taiwan." It was the first time that this award was conferred on a Japanese national.

■ ■ ■ ■ ■

I visited Taiwan for the first time in March 1995, having been invited to attend events commemorating the thirty-third anniversary of the founding of Chinese Culture University. When I entered the sprawling campus on the flank of Mount Yangming just outside Taipei, its ambiance, its beauty and its energetic students and faculty reminded me of Soka University. I also gladly accepted CCU's invitation to the gala celebrating its fortieth anniversary, which was held on March 1, 2002.

The festivities lasted the entire day, with students, alumni and faculty participating together in numerous events. A torchlighting ceremony in front of the on-campus gravesite of the university's founder, Dr. Chang Chi-yun, kicked off the celebration. Chairman Chang ignited the first torch, followed by President Lin, then the faculty, and finally student representatives, until the last torch was lit. A dozen or so torch-bearing students then set out in every direction—running from in front of the gravesite toward various locations on campus and to surrounding towns. To witness this ritual was a moving experience. It symbolized the students and faculty carrying on as one the founding spirit that is the origin of their school.

I am told that when CCU's founder, Dr. Chang, had to be hospitalized in the final days of his life, he asked for a room with a view of his beloved campus. I also heard that his wife frequently joked, "My husband loves the university more than me, and its students more than his own son." Love for the students is the very essence of a founder's spirit, something that perhaps only another university founder can truly grasp.

Chairman Chang and a dozen or so CCU delegates attended the presentation ceremony at Soka University on March 24. Also there were the first chapter leader of the Taipei Chapter, Chu Wan Lee, and more than seventy SGI-Taiwan members. It seemed almost as if the event were taking place in Taiwan.

Forty years after the encounter at Songshan Airport, spring was in full bloom for the Taiwan members. This day's gathering constituted vivid proof that "winter always turns to spring."

Published April 9, 2003

Notes

1. Tokugawa Ieyasu (1543–1616) was a military leader and statesman, founder and first shogun of the Tokugawa Shogunate of Japan, which ruled from 1600 until the Meiji Restoration in 1868. Ieyasu organized new laws to regulate the court and the military clans, and laid the foundations for more than two hundred fifty years of peace under Tokugawa rule during the Edo period (1600–1867), which is also known as the beginning of the early modern period of Japan.
2. Daisaku Ikeda, *The New Human Revolution*, vol. 7 (Santa Monica, CA: World Tribune Press, 2001), pp. 256–62.
3. *The New Human Revolution*, vol. 7, pp. 345–54.

A Great Beacon of Peace and Education

27

Address at the First Entrance Ceremony of Soka University of America in Aliso Viejo, California

First, I offer my heartfelt congratulations on this very first Entrance Ceremony of Soka University of America.

I also extend my welcome and deepest appreciation to all the students in the first class of the undergraduate program of Soka University of America, who have come here from all over the world. And to all of your friends and family members who have joined you here today, congratulations are also in order. Last, but certainly not least, allow me to express my utmost admiration and thanks to the faculty members, who, out of their reverence for the ideals of SUA, gave up prestigious positions at other institutions in order to become teachers at this new university. We entrust you with these precious new students and with SUA itself, knowing that they will be in good hands.

Although it is only appropriate that the founder, my father, Daisaku Ikeda, should deliver his message to you in person, he has regrettably been detained on other business and, try as he might, could not attend today. Therefore, I came from Japan to attend this ceremony on his behalf.

I think it is important to remember that even those schools considered the leading institutions of higher education in the world today had humble beginnings, as we can see by looking into their actual history. Just as a great river, when followed to its source, reveals its origin as a small, obscure spring nestled deep in the mountains, these prominent institutions also got off to very small and unremarkable starts.

Today, we are starting out with one hundred twenty students in the first undergraduate class of SUA. As we continue to move forward, putting our efforts into building up our school, we will certainly look back on this and think what a small start it was indeed. But none of the now-famous universities garnered as much national or international recognition in their initial stages as SUA has today. As you know, SUA has been widely covered in the American media, as the story was introduced by the Associated Press last week and picked up by more than thirty newspapers around the country, starting with the world's leading opinion paper, the *New York Times*. Local television in California also ran a special feature on SUA, which included interviews with faculty and student representatives; this also generated quite a response. In addition, newspapers and magazines in both the United States and Japan are showing an interest in covering the events of today's entrance ceremony.

Why, then, is an unknown university, still without even one student, receiving this much attention? Of course, we owe a great deal of this to the outstanding public relations professionals at SUA, but I firmly believe that at the most basic level, it is proof of the twenty-first century's demand for the humanistic education originated by Tsunesaburo Makiguchi, the father of

Soka education. In addition, it is most unusual for a school to make its start in such an ideal educational environment as has been prepared for us here in Orange County. I know that all of you here today have felt this as you experience it firsthand. I am sure that the world is amazed and intrigued by this as well, which is another reason our school opening is receiving so much attention.

Moreover, this campus did not arise from the investment of one wealthy tycoon; it is the fruit of a labor of love, the contributions of countless ordinary folk who came together in support of the ideals of Soka education. Each little tile, every tiny screw that was used to construct the classrooms you will use, the dormitories, even the cafeteria—none of this would have been possible without the heartfelt contribution of every person who resolved to make this school a reality. Many of these people never had the chance to go to university themselves. Most of them you will never meet, or even know their names. You will probably never encounter those many thousands of people who prepared the land for this campus and who helped in the design and construction of the buildings. Take a minute and picture in your minds the faces of those who worked so hard under the scorching sun in order to have everything prepared in time for your bright new start.

The other day, each of you in the inaugural class of SUA's undergraduate program received a quilt made by members of your local SGI organization here in Orange County. The quilts were the members' way of expressing their heartfelt welcome to the bright students of the first class. Use your imagination and visualize the love and effort that went into the creation of each handmade quilt, stitch by stitch—each a unique design, each a different size.

When Soka University in Japan first opened, the founder, Mr. Ikeda, told the incoming freshmen over and over again to "be creative human beings." Imagination is a key component of creativity. The imagination with which to know, feel and appreciate this sort of altruistic love—a love that goes unseen by the self-centered—cannot emerge from the mere acquisition of knowledge not grounded in solid beliefs.

All of you have embraced this great ideal and hope, and have congregated here from every corner of the world.

Four years from now, when you are ready to graduate, I wonder what answers you will have found in your hearts as you go out into the world. While you are here at school, always keep the question "For what purpose do I study?" fresh in your minds, devote yourselves to your studies, and build lifelong friendships with the faculty and staff, beginning with the founder. At the same time, I hope you will cultivate friendships with your classmates and with those younger students who will enter the school after you.

Lastly, from the bottom of my heart, I pray that you will enjoy a comfortable, bright and wonderfully fun-filled time here at school. Enjoy your youth by living your lives to the fullest—that is my wish for you.

Presented August 24, 2001, at Soka University of America, Aliso Viejo

28

Visiting Morehouse College, the Sanctuary of Civil Rights

On April 7, 2002, I visited America's prestigious Morehouse College in Atlanta, a year after my first visit to the campus. This trip I made on behalf of my father, SGI President Daisaku Ikeda, whom the college was to award an honorary doctorate of humane letters. I accepted the diploma and a Morehouse College doctoral hood from the school's president, Dr. Walter E. Massey, whom I was happy to meet again. Morehouse College is the alma mater of Dr. Martin Luther King Jr. (Class of 1948). Every January and April, a ceremony to honor Dr. King's contributions to civil rights and peace is held on campus in the grand auditorium of the Martin Luther King Jr. International Chapel, which was established to carry on Dr. King's legacy.

The Gandhi, King, Ikeda Community Builders Prize,[1] conceptualized by the dean of the Martin Luther King Jr. International Chapel, Dr. Lawrence Edward Carter Sr., was established last year (2001). Prince El Hassan bin Talal of Jordan was the first to receive the award, for his efforts toward peace in the Middle East. Prince Hassan is president of the Club of Rome,[2] and a member of the Royal Family of Jordan, recognized as direct descendants of Mohammed, the founder of Islam.

This year, the award went to Dr. Michael Nobel, chairman of the Nobel Family Society[3] and chairman of the board of the Appeal of the Nobel Peace Laureates Foundation.[4]

Prince Hassan mentioned when I met him last year that he was well aware of my father's deep friendships with Dr. Aurelio Peccei, founder of the Club of Rome, and Dr. Ricardo Díez-Hochleitner, its former president. He spoke candidly about his affinity with the SGI, and his generous words touched me deeply.

This year's recipient, Dr. Michael Nobel, is quite familiar with my father's writings, I was surprised to learn. And when Dr. Nobel offered me his family nameplate, a valuable symbol of the distinguished history of the Nobel family, to present to my father, I was moved all the more. But I respectfully declined his offer. "That nameplate is a testament to your family's honor," I said. "Please accept my thanks for your generous gesture, but I cannot accept something so priceless." But Dr. Nobel insisted, "I would be most appreciative if you would deliver it to your father." Once again he offered the nameplate, which this time I gratefully accepted.

The first SGI member that Dr. Carter ever encountered was a member of the SGI-USA women's division who taught at a nearby university. Likewise, Dr. Nobel learned of SGI-USA's Victory Over Violence program through a friendship he developed with an SGI-USA women's division member in Florida. Encounters such as these reassure me that SGI's diverse network of peace, culture, education and human rights is developing on a global scale, through the earnest efforts of determined individuals.

When I think of it, it's clear that my father, too, has opened the way for understanding around the world through his ongoing treatment of others with sincerity and friendship grounded in their shared humanity. And today we see many disciples around the globe taking responsibility to carry on this legacy. The shared struggle of mentor and disciples continues to develop even as the world today is shrinking.

The exhibition "Gandhi, King, Ikeda—A Legacy of Building Peace" came home to the Martin Luther King Jr. International Chapel after a one-year absence. It was on display in the Chapel lobby during the award ceremony. When Dr. Carter first told me of his idea to include the name *Ikeda* in this exhibition, I was perplexed. Through the years, my father has been introducing the words, deeds and ideas of Mahatma Gandhi and Dr. Martin Luther King Jr. as model leaders who gave their all for the good of the people. But he never entertained the thought that his name would one day be mentioned in the same breath as these two great men.

Dr. Carter offered me these words, which touched me deeply: "Introducing the life of SGI President Ikeda in this exhibition will allow the American people to understand correctly the Buddhist ideal of humanism as a grassroots movement inherited from presidents Makiguchi and Toda, as well as the ideal of world peace that the SGI is striving to attain. These ideals strongly resonate with, and can support a deeper understanding of, the ideals of Mahatma Gandhi and Dr. King." In the past year, the "Gandhi, King, Ikeda" exhibition has toured more than twenty US cities and has been experienced by more than one hundred and fifty thousand people.

Dr. Carter and those affiliated with Morehouse College share with the Soka Gakkai no common religious or cultural origin, yet their deep understanding and compassionate support of the SGI in promoting its Buddhism-based world peace movement is most encouraging. They made my trip to Atlanta a truly memorable experience.

Published in the May 11, 2002, *Seikyo Shimbun*

Notes

1. The Gandhi, King, Ikeda Community Builders Prize, conceptualized by the dean of the Martin Luther King Jr. International Chapel, Dr. Lawrence Edward Carter Sr., was established in 2001. The prize is awarded to individuals making dynamic efforts for peace.
2. Club of Rome—In April 1968, an international group of professionals from the fields of diplomacy, industry, academia and civil society met at a quiet villa in Rome. Invited by Italian industrialist Aurelio Peccei and Scottish scientist Alexander King, they came together to discuss the dilemma of prevailing short-term thinking in international affairs and, in particular, the concerns regarding unlimited resource consumption in an increasingly interdependent world. Dr. Ricardo Díez-Hochleitner was president of the Club of Rome from 1991 to 2000. See http://www.clubofrome.org
3. Nobel Family Society—The society of family members of Nobel Prize founder Dr. Alfred Nobel.
4. Appeal of the Nobel Peace Laureates Foundation—Also known as The Peace Appeal Foundation. It is an organization that promotes peace and conflict resolution through consistent and direct mediation, facilitation and advisory services. Its approach to conflict is dynamic and multidimensional. The foundation was established in response to the United Nations International Decade for a Culture of Peace and Non-violence for the Children of the World, by some of the same Nobel Peace laureates who designated the United Nations decade as such.

29

Soka University of America: Crystallizing the People's Sincerity

On April 4 (2002), before flying to Atlanta, Georgia, to visit Morehouse College, I had the opportunity to tour the campus of Soka University of America in Aliso Viejo, California. My first visit had been eight months earlier, when I attended the university's first entrance ceremony, on August 24, 2001.

The trees and grass on campus had turned a deeper hue, and a sea of poppies, California's state flower, added a touch of springtime gold to the green of the school landscape.

The students of the first entering class had seemed a bit nervous when I met with them last August. But this time around, I was very happy to see them exerting themselves in their studies with freedom and ease as they assumed their lead role at the university. Some classes had midterm examinations that day, so I could not meet every student. But whenever I passed them on campus, I noticed that their faces seemed to glow with vitality. One professor told me that last semester the focus had been on humanities-related curricula that required English proficiency, so the foreign students went through a much tougher time than the others. But in the current semester, the focus was more math- and science-related, disciplines at which students from Japan tended to excel.

In just the short time since its opening, SUA has welcomed a host of world-renowned scholars and academics, including presidents of various universities from all over the globe, each of whom graciously took time to speak with our inquisitive students. Among them was the 1995 Nobel Peace laureate and cofounder of the Pugwash Conferences on Science and World Affairs,[1] Sir Joseph Rotblat. There is probably no more inspiring lesson for young students than to interact directly with great thinkers of the world.

The September 11 terrorist attacks happened almost immediately after SUA's first semester started. The students held a dialogue meeting that day, where they decided to sponsor and invite local residents to a community candlelight vigil at the Peace Fountain on campus to be held that evening. Students and others from the community gathered at SUA to offer prayers for those who lost their lives in the attacks and to deepen and reinforce their awareness of the importance of peace.

The event drew much interest, and a local newspaper covered it with a long article. Even more significant was the fact that the students had taken the initiative to create this event. It was an opportunity for interaction on a personal, human level between the university and residents of the local community. Their actions won high praise both on and off campus.

Since then, SUA students have launched a student government, formed a number of student clubs and made great strides in building a student-centered university, an important ideal of Soka education.

Another aspect that deeply touched me was the faculty, who, having come to SUA to support the Soka educational philosophy, are working selflessly for the good of the students. The United States has a practical employment culture that is based on contract law. Once offered a job, for example, a person enters into employment only after a job description and compensation have been made absolutely clear. Universities are no exception to such conventions. But in the behavior and demeanor of the SUA faculty and staff, I sensed a willingness to do work far beyond the call of duty. All are passionate and proactive, determined and glad to do whatever it takes to benefit the students. It impressed me to hear that the cafeteria workers, for example, pay very close attention to dietary health, and by adjusting flavors and seasoning, they work hard to respond to the tastes and eating habits of an internationally diverse student body.

Moreover, I am told that when the first class moved into its dormitories last year, the faculty, including SUA President Daniel Habuki, worked up quite a sweat carrying each student's heavy suitcases to the dorm rooms. The scene moved family members who witnessed it, evoking statements like "I never knew a university like this existed!" President Habuki told me: "I'm only putting into action what I learned from the founder of Soka University, Mr. Ikeda, when I was in the first class of Soka University in Japan. It's my way of repaying my gratitude to him."

The first Soka Gakkai president, Tsunesaburo Makiguchi, and second president, Josei Toda, were compassionate educators. Soka education takes their spirit as its source. Today, united by the university founder's grand vision, the disciples are enabling that spirit to flourish in this great land of America.

Soka University of America is a university created by the people—the crystallization of ordinary people's devotion. In response to the people's wishes, we have now begun the process of university building—a cooperative effort among students, faculty and staff who are determined to proceed with the same spirit and passion for education as their founder. And it gives me great pleasure to report this to our supporters around the world.

Published in the May 15, 2002, *Seikyo Shimbun*

Notes

1. The Pugwash Conferences on Science and World Affairs take their name from the village of Pugwash, Nova Scotia, Canada, birthplace of the American philanthropist Cyrus Eaton, who hosted the first conference there in 1957. That gathering was inspired by a manifesto issued in 1955 by Bertrand Russell and Albert Einstein, which called upon scientists of all political persuasions to assemble to discuss the threat posed by thermonuclear weapons. The Pugwash Conferences bring together world scholars and public figures concerned with reducing armed conflict and seeking cooperative solutions for global problems.

30

Address at the Second Entrance Ceremony of Soka University of America in Aliso Viejo, California

From the bottom of my heart, I congratulate the members of the class of 2006 who have gathered here today in the brilliant Southern California sunshine. Today, at this magnificent campus, you embark on a new journey of scholarship and character building. Permit me also to congratulate the families and friends of the students. From here, your smiles look even brighter than today's beautiful blue sky.

On behalf of my father, Daisaku Ikeda, the founder of Soka University of America, I would like to convey our deepest thanks to everyone—to the distinguished faculty and staff, the trustees and of course the students of the class of 2005; to all who have worked so selflessly over the past year to build the foundations for SUA's educational experience. My father had very much hoped to attend today's ceremony. In the end, however, it proved impossible for him to travel outside Japan at this juncture, and he asked me to attend as his representative. He also entrusted me with his message on this occasion, which will be shared with us later in the ceremony.

My father, as you know, has made education his life's work, and his greatest wish has been to visit SUA at the very earliest opportunity. Last year and this year, as well, he has welcomed and met whenever possible with representatives of what is now the sophomore class, the faculty and the staff, when they have visited Japan. I have witnessed how much he has enjoyed these interactions—more, it would seem, than with anyone else in the world—and the way that he has poured heart and soul into offering encouragement to the students of SUA. Just the other day, members of the SUA student government association were visiting Japan to conduct exchanges with their counterparts at Soka University in Hachioji, Tokyo. In a meeting that was later broadcast nationwide, he introduced to the audience, with great joy and pride, the SUA student representatives. Many who watched the broadcast throughout Japan have commented that this scene moved them deeply.

SUA enjoys the support of a network of outstanding individuals, united in their commitment to the ideal of education. Here I would like to acknowledge our very special guests Dr. Jules Brassner and his wife, San Lee, and the Honorable Mayor Carmen Vali-Cave of the City of Aliso Viejo. Globally, SUA counts among its friends and supporters such renowned figures as Nobel Laureate Dr. Joseph Rotblat, Dr. Linus Pauling Jr., Dr. Arun Gandhi and Dr. Michael Nobel, all of whom kindly visited SUA in the days immediately following its opening. It was almost as if they could hardly wait for the school to open before visiting the campus and speaking here. I would like to take this opportunity to thank all our special guests and all of you who extend to SUA your unwavering support.

As I mentioned at last year's entrance ceremony, I believe a true source of pride for SUA is the support we receive from ordinary people throughout the world who regard the ideals of Soka education as an embodiment of their hopes and dreams.

Whenever SUA President Habuki travels, whether within the United States or abroad, he makes a special effort to meet with the university's donors. He does so to thank them and to keep them up-to-date on the development of the university. This spring, when he was in Osaka, Japan, Dr. Habuki went to visit the home of a woman who had made an extremely generous donation to the university. As he looked for her residence, he imagined the kind of palatial home that might belong to a person of such means. He found himself struggling to locate her home based on the address he had been given. Contrary to his expectations, she lived in a very small and simple home—so unobtrusive that he had walked right past it.

When he had finally managed to find the house with that address, he noticed a neatly dressed woman standing in front hanging out laundry. Still unsure, he asked if he had the right address. And indeed, she turned out to be the donor who had made that very generous gift to the university. In her words: "I don't need to live in luxury. Nothing gives me greater joy than to be able to help President Ikeda realize his educational vision."

Last year, volunteers in Orange County quilted blankets—one for each member of the undergraduate class of 2005. This year, I understand, they have made hand-knitted mufflers for the members of the new class of 2006. One such volunteer, because of her very demanding schedule, could only knit a few rows per day, and so it took her six months to complete the muffler. These friends of the university had noted that in winter this hilltop campus is exposed to chilly winds. Hearing how members of the class of 2005 were studying late at night in the library, wrapped in the quilts to keep warm, they decided to make mufflers to help students of the class of 2006 stay warm, as well.

All of us here today should be deeply aware of the sincerity of the many, many people who are extending SUA their support. For us, Soka education means always remembering and appreciating the sincerity and kindness of others.

In the words of a great Eastern philosopher, when you light a lamp for another, your own way will be lit. I was deeply moved to learn that, without any particular direction from the faculty, many students last year took the initiative to study with fellow classmates for whom English is a second language, helping them overcome their disadvantage as non-native speakers. In doing this, they willingly sacrificed their own precious study time.

Empathy for the struggles of another—this, above all, is the heart of global citizenship, to which SUA aspires. I sincerely hope and trust that such compassionate action will become a firmly established tradition at SUA, that it will be carefully nurtured and passed on from the members of one class to the next.

John Steinbeck, the Nobel Prize-winning novelist, was born one hundred years ago here in California. In the essay that proved to be his final literary work, "America and Americans," he explores the nature of civilization. As a culminating expression of his years as a writer and his deep love for his country, he considers the nature of the challenges that forged the spirit of the American people. "Maybe the challenge was in the land," he wrote, "or it might be that the people made the challenge."[1]

I believe that the same can be said today. In the challenges that await you on the grand stage of our world, and in the courage with which you meet those challenges, the spirit of genuine global citizenship will be honed and forged. Next year, members of the class of 2005 will spend a semester abroad. They will be followed soon after by this year's freshman class. To gather people of talent from throughout the world; to contribute people of talent and vision to the world—this is the dream of SUA that I believe you, through your determined efforts, will make a reality. I close by offering my heartfelt wishes that your future be filled with limitless success and glory. Again, congratulations!

Presented August 17, 2002, at Soka University of America, Aliso Viejo

Note

1. John Steinbeck, *America and Americans and Selected Nonfiction* (New York: The Penguin Group, 2002), p. 403.

31

My Memory of Dunhuang, a Treasure of the World

O N OCTOBER 8 this year (2003), Northwest Normal University of China awarded my father an honorary professorship. Last year, that university, a prestigious teacher training institution, celebrated its centennial.

Northwest Normal University was founded originally in Beijing. But with the outbreak of war with Japan, in order to avoid invading Japanese troops, the university moved in 1937 to Lanzhou in Gansu Province, some six hundred twenty miles away.

Lanzhou was, since ancient times, a key trading post along the Silk Road, and the Yellow River flows through the city's center. Northwest Normal University has conducted extensive research into the art of Dunhuang, a town on the old Silk Road famous for its caves filled with Buddhist artworks. In his speech at the conferral of the honorary professorship,[1] university president Dr. Wang Limin commended my father's enduring commitment to the protection and study of the art at Dunhuang.

■ ■ ■ ■ ■

My father, it seems, has had a fascination with Dunhuang since childhood. His fifth-grade teacher, pointing to a large world map hanging in the classroom, once asked him where he would like to go in the future. My father answered that he would love to visit the desert of China's interior.

The Sino-Japanese War had just begun, and perhaps his interest in China stemmed from the fact that his four elder brothers had been sent into military service there and in other war zones in Asia.

The teacher said, "In the desert where you said you want to go, there is a place called Dunhuang that is filled with many wonderful treasures."

Thinking it wondrous that such treasures should be found in the desert, my father cherished in his heart a romantic image of Dunhuang.

Drawing on this memory, he later wrote a children's story, "A Treasure Castle in the Desert," in which a man called Uncle Zhou dedicates himself to protecting artworks in the desert. He modeled the character Uncle Zhou on Mr. Chang Shuhong.

■ ■ ■ ■ ■

Mr. Chang studied painting in Paris while in his twenties, and showed great promise as a Western-style artist. It was in Paris that he first learned of the paintings in the Mogao Caves of Dunhuang. He resolved to go see them, and for half a century thereafter devoted his life to protecting and studying the art of Dunhuang. Indeed, Mr. Chang Shuhong is known as the protector of Dunhuang.

Mr. Chang was more than twenty years my father's senior. Yet, my father first heard of Dunhuang from his fifth-grade teacher at just about the same time Mr. Chang became aware of it while in Paris—an interesting coincidence.

The two men met for the first time in 1980, when Mr. Chang was director of the Dunhuang Research Institute. They spoke joyfully during that first encounter, like longtime close friends. Their dialogues continued after that, and in 1990 were published as a book titled *The Splendor of Dunhuang*.

■ ■ ■ ■ ■

I developed my own interest in Dunhuang through reading the novel *Dunhuang* by Yasushi Inoue and also by watching a television documentary series on the Silk Road that ran on Japan's national broadcasting network. The program's theme song actually became quite popular. The Kansai Soka Schools, while I was teaching there, even adopted the melody to play on the campus public address system in order to signal the end of each school day. I would listen to the tune drifting through the school hallways, as the sky took on twilight hues, and dream of the Silk Road stretching far out beyond the sunset. That dream came true sooner than I could have imagined.

In the summer of 1984, I had the opportunity to tour the Silk Road as a member of a Soka Schools delegation to China, which consisted mainly of social studies faculty from the Tokyo and Kansai Soka Schools. My brother Takahiro, then a teacher at the Kansai Soka Elementary School, also joined us.

We visited ten cities in twenty-five days, covering about seventy-five hundred miles, and our visit to Dunhuang was most memorable. Just before we left Japan, my father had published a book titled *My Thoughts on Dunhuang*. As I read it during our travels, I grew all the more excited about what we would find there.

Today a direct flight from Beijing to Dunhuang takes about three hours. In those days, however, passenger flights were not permitted to use the Dunhuang airport, which was open only to military aircraft. To reach Dunhuang, we had to fly three hours from Beijing to Lanzhou by propeller plane, and another two-and-a-half hours from Lanzhou to Jiuquan on a smaller propeller plane. We then traveled by bus from Jiuquan to Dunhuang.

Our bus left Jiuquan at eight on the morning of July 29, and took us across the Gobi Desert. Though the bus was air-conditioned, the temperature inside rose to more than eighty-six degrees Fahrenheit. From the bus window we saw an unbroken, sweeping landscape of gravel soil and brown, rocky mountains. I imagined with awe how it must have been for the Tripitaka Master Xuanzang[2] as he traversed this rough terrain in search of Buddhism. We arrived at the greenery-wrapped oasis of Dunhuang at around sunset, after six o'clock. That evening I introduced to the members of our delegation a message my father had asked me to share with them upon reaching Dunhuang. It included this poem:

In Dunhuang
Where history shines brilliantly
You hoist your banner
At long last.

Daisaku
July 29, 1984

■ ■ ■ ■ ■

Dun of Dunhuang means "grand," and *huang* means "to shine." UNESCO has designated it a world cultural heritage site. I feel it is very fitting that Dunhuang be recognized in this way as a global treasure, a grand and shining beacon for humanity. Behind the recognition it currently enjoys have been the ongoing painstaking efforts of truly dedicated individuals like Mr. Chang.

Mr. Chang once told my father: "Each time I meet you, I am deeply moved in a way that stirs my very soul. This is because you have fought for world peace, for culture and art, and for friendship between China and Japan, overcoming every criticism and obstacle along the way. And this causes me to reflect on the struggles I have waged in my own life. In the quest for an ideal, one must face opposition and difficulties that are unseen to others. To achieve anything great, we must continuously face one bitter hardship after another, though no one else is aware. Judging from my own experience, you must have had to undergo immense hardships in carrying out such great work. When I think about it, my heart fills with a thousand emotions."

■ ■ ■ ■ ■

In June 1984, the month before we finished our tour of the Silk Road, my father made his sixth visit to China, during which he received honorary professorships from Peking and Fudan universities. These were the first two honorary titles awarded him by Chinese academic institutions. With the honorary degree from Northwest Normal University, the awards he has received from Chinese institutions over the past nineteen years number fifty-two, while his honorary academic titles from around the world total 145.[3]

Attending the Northwest Normal University conferral ceremony, I reflected on what we must do: By earnestly moving, working, speaking and fighting for our ideals, we can build our own enduring city like Dunhuang, a treasure house of peace and victory.

> Published in the October 22, 2003, *Koko Shimpo*, the Soka Gakkai's high school division newspaper

Notes

1. Northwest Normal University of China awarded SGI President Ikeda an honorary professorship at a ceremony held at the Soka International Friendship Hall in Sendagaya, Tokyo, on October 8, 2003.
2. Xuanzang (602–664) (*Hsüan-tsang* in Wade-Giles Romanization; Jpn *Genjo*) —A Chinese priest and a translator of Buddhist scriptures known for his travels through Central Asia and India. He recorded his seventeen-year journey through India and Central Asia in *The Record of the Western Regions*, the most comprehensive account of its kind ever written in the Orient. Upon returning to China, he devoted the rest of his life to translating Buddhist texts he had brought with him and to the teaching of Buddhism. The Chinese literary classic *Journey to the West* was inspired by Xuanzang's travels.
3. As of July 2008, there have been more than 240 academic titles conferred upon SGI President Daisaku Ikeda from institutions of higher learning throughout the world.

32

On China's Manned Spaceflight

I HAD JUST written my previous essay titled "My Memory of Dunhuang, a Treasure of the World" when news broke of China's October 15 (2003) launch of its first manned spacecraft. The launch was made from the Jiuquan Satellite Launch Center.

Jiuquan, a city of several hundred thousand, is small by Chinese standards. Once a crucial hub along the Silk Road, it prospered through trade with the West. Jiuquan is now the gateway to Dunhuang,[1] and I remember it well as the place where our party boarded a bus for that historic site. The space launch suddenly thrust the name *Jiuquan* into the spotlight. (The Jiuquan Launch Center, however, is in the Inner Mongolian Autonomous Region, about 125 miles from central Jiuquan.)

■ ■ ■ ■ ■

Dunhuang has as its symbol a mythological celestial maiden known as *Apsaras* in Sanskrit and as *Feitian* in Chinese. Her image, with robes fluttering in the heavens, can be seen in paintings and sculptures all around town, a tribute to the many such beings portrayed in the paintings found in Dunhuang's Mogao Caves. According to Mr. Chang Shuhong, then the director of the Dunhuang Research Institute, images of Apsaras, large and small, are found in some 270 of the 492 caves comprising Mogao.

The work of creating the Mogao Caves began in the fourth century and continued for nearly one thousand years, and so how the floating Apsaras were depicted naturally differed from era to era. While generally regarded as female, those appearing in some of the cave paintings are male. In a sense we could view Yang Liwei, the first Chinese man in space, as a modern personification of the Apsaras.

China's next space program, the Chang'e project, aims to explore the moon's surface. *Chang'e* is the name of a Chinese mythological goddess who flew to the moon and remained there. It seems that, at the spot on the Silk Road where the civilizations of East and West once met, projects to soar to the reaches of space are making steady progress.[2]

■ ■ ■ ■ ■ ■

The Chinese characters that form the name *Mogao* suggest a high point in the midst of nothingness. The cluster of caves, carved into the face of a sandstone cliff on Mount Mingsha, rises above surrounding desert. Viewed from a distance, the hillside with its many cave entrances resembles a giant honeycomb. Without venturing inside, one would never guess that these caves house treasures of Buddhist art.

All of the caves face east, and natural light illuminates their interiors for only a brief time each morning. When we toured the caves, we had to depend on flashlights. I deeply respect the imaginative power and tenacity of those unknown artists who created the remarkably colorful paintings in these dark caves.

Was it not religious passion that enabled the artists of Dunhuang to create these masterpieces amid such adverse circumstances? It must have been their Buddhist faith that allowed them to maximize their innate artistic talents and create impressive works that would inspire people for generations into the future.

■ ■ ■ ■

The success of the manned space mission, I learned, stemmed from improvements China had made to technology gained from the former Soviet Union. Among the capable individuals instrumental to that success were many graduates of Shanghai Jiao Tong University.

Founded more than a century ago, Shanghai Jiao Tong University ranks with Peking (Beijing) and Tianjin universities as one of China's oldest. Former President of the People's Republic of China Jiang Zemin and Dr. Qian Xuesen, who is known as the father of China's space program, are among its graduates.

About a week after the launch, a ceremony to confer upon my father the title of honorary professor of Shanghai Jiao Tong University was conducted with the university's vice president, Dr. Zhang Shengkun, and other university representatives attending.[3] My father, in his acceptance address, heartily commended the success of the launch, observing that "this victory in spaceflight signifies the victory of your university."

The key to a successful space launch lies in the attainment of "escape velocity." This entails burning the spacecraft's engines at full thrust from liftoff until it develops enough speed to escape the atmosphere and overcome the pull of Earth's gravity.

I think a similar principle applies to our lives.

If, when it comes time to take action, we do so only halfheartedly, we will never enter the orbit of a winning life. On the other hand, those who apply all their energy when necessary, burning their engines at full power, so to speak, will definitely win.

I pray that you, the members of the high school division, will challenge yourselves to apply "full thrust" in everything you do while young and prepare for the day when you will soar aloft as outstanding leaders of the twenty-first century.

Pubished in the November 12, 2003, Koko Shimpo,
the Soka Gakkai's high school division newspaper

Notes

1. Dunhuang is a town on the old Silk Road famous for its caves filled with Buddhist artworks.
2. Chang'e 1 lunar orbiter was successfully launched October 24, 2007, from the Xichang launch center in Sichuan province, China.
3. Shanghai Jiao Tong University awarded SGI President Ikeda an honorary professorship at a ceremony held at the Soka International Friendship Hall in Sendagaya, Tokyo, on October 24, 2003.

Postscript

THERE IS a story I heard from my father when I was in the sixth grade. At the time, we lived in a small, very modest house in Kobayashi-cho, in Tokyo's Ota Ward. It often happened that those who came to visit, thinking that such a tiny house could never belong to the Soka Gakkai president, would often walk right past it, expecting to find a more opulent dwelling further on. But for me it was our precious home, a place of countless dear and unforgettable memories.

One day, just after I had entered the sixth grade, my father spoke to me as we took in the sunlight on our small veranda. My mother looked on, with her gentle, youthful smile, at this exchange between father and son. I remember having trouble hearing him because of the loud voices of children playing in the neighborhood. He said to me quietly, yet powerfully: "Your name, *Hiromasa*, was given to you by President Toda, who said: 'I would like to see him grow up to become a man of letters or an educator. I hope he will become a person whose writings live on.'"

My mother nodded and said, "Yes, that is true." And so until now I have lived with the thought that I must one day set down something in writing in order to respond to President Toda's expectations and also to my parents' wishes.

When I was in college, I practiced writing from time to time. But I became so busy with extracurricular and Soka Gakkai activities that I never took the time to fully savor the experience of writing, something I regret to this day.

As a senior to the future division, I wanted to provide younger members with even a little nourishment for their development. With that in mind, I began contributing essays to the *Koko Shimpo*, the Soka Gakkai's high school division newspaper, and have continued to do so for several years now.

An unexpected request came from the publishing company Otorisyoin, and a number of these essays now appear in this book, *My Path of Youth*. If, through publishing this book, I have in some small way responded to President Toda's expectations of me, then I am truly pleased. My parents offered encouragement, telling me: "Even if your writing is unpolished, if it would make President Toda happy, you should do it. That is because leaving a record of the truth, exactly as it is, in itself is a noble act."

I am resolved to continue honing my writing skills as a tool for good, for the sake of our late mentor, Josei Toda, for our precious younger members and for myself.

In conclusion, I extend my sincerest thanks to Chief Editor Yoshiyuki Okamoto of the *Koko Shimpo* for his support in serializing my essays, and to the leaders of the high school division, past and present, including Mr. Tadayuki Ishiguro.

Hiromasa Ikeda
June 7, 2003, on the fortieth anniversary of the
establishment of the Soka Gakkai high school division

More on Nichiren Buddhism and Its Application to Daily Life

The following twelve titles can be purchased from your local or online bookseller, or go to the Middleway Press Web site (www.middlewaypress.com).

The Buddha in Your Mirror: Practical Buddhism and the Search for Self, by Woody Hochswender, Greg Martin and Ted Morino
A best-selling Buddhist primer that reveals the most modern, effective and practical way to achieve what is called enlightenment or Buddhahood. Based on the centuries-old teaching of the Japanese Buddhist master Nichiren, this method has been called the "direct path" to enlightenment.
(Paperback: ISBN 978-0-9674697-8-2; $14.00, Hardcover: ISBN 978-0-9674697-1-3; $23.95)

The Buddha Next Door:
Ordinary People, Extraordinary Stories
by Zan Gaudioso and Greg Martin
This anthology of personal experiences illuminates how the practice of Nichiren Buddhism has changed people's lives for the better. These

first-person narratives—representing people from throughout the country of various ages and ethnic backgrounds—examine the challenges of daily life associated with health, relationships, career and aging, and the ensuing experiences of hope, success, inspiration and personal enlightenment that come about as a result of living as Nichiren Buddhists.
(Paperback: ISBN 978-0-9779245-1-6; $15.95)

Buddhism Day by Day: Wisdom for Modern Life
by Daisaku Ikeda
This treasury of practical information and encouragement will appeal to those seeking a deeper understanding of how to apply the tenets of Nichiren Buddhism in their day-to-day lives.
(Paperback: ISBN 978-0-9723267-5-9; $15.95)

Buddhism for You series
In this oasis of insight and advice on the power of Nichiren Buddhism—which holds that everyone has a Buddha nature of limitless power, wisdom and compassion—readers will learn how to live a life filled with courage, determination, love and prayer to achieve their goals and desires.

(**Courage** Hardcover: ISBN 978-0-9723267-6-6; $7.95)
(**Determination** Hardcover: ISBN 978-0-9723267-8-0; $7.95)
(**Love** Hardcover: ISBN 978-0-9723267-7-3; $7.95)
(**Prayer** Hardcover: ISBN 978-0-9723267-9-7; $7.95)

Choose Hope: Your Role in Waging Peace in the Nuclear Age,
by David Krieger and Daisaku Ikeda
"In this nuclear age, when the future of humankind is imperiled by irrational strategies, it is imperative to restore sanity to our policies and hope to our destiny. Only a rational analysis of our problems

can lead to their solution. This book is an example par excellence of a rational approach."
—Joseph Rotblat, Nobel Peace Prize laureate
(Hardcover: ISBN 978-0-9674697-6-8; $23.95)

Planetary Citizenship: *Your* Values, Beliefs and Actions *Can* Shape a Sustainable World
by Hazel Henderson and Daisaku Ikeda
"*Planetary Citizenship* is a delightful introduction to some of the most important ideas and facts concerning stewardship of the planet. I cannot think of any book that deals with more important issues."
—Mihaly Csikszentmihalyi, author of *Flow: The Psychology of Optimal Experience,* California
(Hardcover: ISBN 978-0-9723267-2-8; $23.95)

Romancing the Buddha: Embracing Buddhism in My Everyday Life by Michael Lisagor
"*Romancing the Buddha: Embracing Buddhism in My Everyday Life* is…a resource which provides excellent insights into applying Nichiren Buddhism to the difficulties of daily life, including depression, spousal illness, the challenge of raising two daughters and the quest for happiness. An absorbing and inspirational selection of vignettes touched with wisdom, *Romancing the Buddha* is an impressive and welcome contribution to Buddhist Studies reading lists."
—Midwest Book Review
(Paperback: ISBN 978-0-9723267-4-2; $18.95)

Unlocking the Mysteries of Birth & Death… and Everything In Between, A Buddhist View of Life
(second edition) by Daisaku Ikeda
"In this slender volume, Ikeda presents a wealth of profound

information in a clear and straightforward style that can be easily absorbed by the interested lay reader. His life's work, and the underlying purpose of his book, is simply to help human beings derive maximum meaning from their lives through the study of Buddhism."
—ForeWord Magazine
(Paperback: ISBN 978-0-9723267-0-4; $15.00)

The Way of Youth: Buddhist Common Sense for Handling Life's Questions, by Daisaku Ikeda
"[This book] shows the reader how to flourish as a young person in the world today; how to build confidence and character in modern society; learn to live with respect for oneself and others; how to contribute to a positive, free and peaceful society; and find true personal happiness."
—Midwest Book Review
(Paperback: ISBN 978-0-9674697-0-6; $14.95)

The following World Tribune Press titles can be purchased at SGI-USA bookstores nationwide or through the mail order center: call 800-626-1313 or e-mail mailorder@sgi-usa.org.

Faith into Action: Thoughts on Selected Topics,
by Daisaku Ikeda
A collection of inspirational excerpts arranged by subject. Perfect for finding just the right quote to encourage yourself or a friend or when preparing for a meeting.
(World Tribune Press, mail order #4135; $12.95)

The Human Revolution, boxed set by Daisaku Ikeda
"A great human revolution in just a single individual will help achieve a change in the destiny of a nation, and further, can even enable a change in the destiny of all humankind." With this as his main theme, the author wrote his twelve-volume account of Josei Toda's life and the phenomenal growth of the Soka Gakkai in postwar Japan. Published in a slightly abridged two-book set, this work paints a fascinating and empowering story of the far-reaching effects of one person's inner determination. Josei Toda's awakening and transformation, his efforts to teach others the unlimited power of faith, his dedication in leading thousands out of misery and poverty, the efforts of his devoted disciple Shin'ichi Yamamoto— within these stories we find the keys for building lives of genuine happiness.
(World Tribune Press, mail order #4182; $45.00)

The Journey Begins: First Steps in Buddhist Practice
A pamphlet on the basics of Nichiren Daishonin's Buddhism. Each step is discussed in very basic terms, but each plays an important role in your practice. For the new member, the points will help you build a foundation in your practice. Return to them again and

again throughout your practice to help keep yourself on track and get the maximum benefit from your Buddhist practice.
(World Tribune Press, $1.00 per pamphlet)
[Chinese] mail order #4186
[English] mail order #4138
[French] mail order #4188
[Japanese] mail order #4193
[Spanish] mail order #4139

Kaneko's Story: A Conversation with Kaneko Ikeda
Kaneko Ikeda shares thoughts and stories of her youth, marriage and family and of supporting her husband of more than fifty-five years, SGI President Daisaku Ikeda. Also included are four messages written to the women of the SGI.
(World Tribune Press, mail order #234302; $9.95)

My Dear Friends in America, by Daisaku Ikeda
This volume brings together for the first time all of the SGI president's speeches to US members in the 1990s.
(World Tribune Press, Hardcover: mail order #4104; $19.95)

The New Human Revolution, by Daisaku Ikeda
An ongoing novelized history of the Soka Gakkai, which contains not only episodes from the past but guidance in faith that we can apply as we grow our movement here in the United States.
(World Tribune Press; $12.00 each volume)
Volume 1, mail order #4601
Volume 2, mail order #4602
Volume 3, mail order #4603
Volume 4, mail order #4604
Volume 5, mail order #4605
Volume 6, mail order #4606
Volume 7, mail order #4607
Volume 8, mail order #4608
Volume 9, mail order #4609

Volume 10, mail order #4610
Volume 11, mail order #4611
Volume 12, mail order #4612
Volume 13, mail order #4613
Volume 14, mail order #4614
Volume 15, mail order #275446

The Winning Life:
An Introduction to Buddhist Practice
Using plain language, this booklet gives a quick-yet-detailed introduction to a winning way of life based on Nichiren Daishonin's teachings. A perfect tool for introducing others to the benefits of practice.
(World Tribune Press, $1.00 per booklet)
[Armenian] mail order #4189
[Chinese] mail order #4107
[English] mail order #4105
[French] mail order #4187
[Japanese] mail order #4815
[Korean] mail order #4113
[Spanish] mail order #4106

The Wisdom of the Lotus Sutra, vols. I–VI, by Daisaku Ikeda, Katsuji Saito, Takanori Endo and Haruo Suda
A captivating dialogue on the twenty-eight-chapter Lotus Sutra that brings this ancient writing's important messages into practical application for daily life and for realizing a peaceful world.
(World Tribune Press, $10.95 per volume)
Volume I, mail order #4281
Volume II, mail order #4282
Volume III, mail order #4283
Volume IV, mail order #4284
Volume V, mail order #4285
Volume VI, mail order #4286

The World of Nichiren Daishonin's Writings, vols 1–4,
by Daisaku Ikeda, Katsuji Saito and Masaaki Morinaka
These books bring to life the teachings and major life events of Nichiren Daishonin through an ongoing discussion between SGI President Ikeda, Soka Gakkai Study Department Leader Katsuji Saito and Study Department Vice Leader Masaaki Morinaka. Revitalize our pursuit of creating happiness and peace with this four-volume series.
(SGI Malaysia, $7.95 per volume)
Volume 1, mail order #1891
Volume 2, mail order #1892
Volume 3, mail order #1893
Volume 4, mail order #1894

A Youthful Diary: One Man's Journey From the Beginning of Faith to Worldwide Leadership for Peace, by Daisaku Ikeda
Youthful inspiration for people of all ages. Through the tale of the ever-deepening relationship between the young Daisaku Ikeda and his mentor-in-life, Josei Toda, *A Youthful Diary* is a compelling account of both triumphs and setbacks on the road to establishing the foundation of today's Soka Gakkai.
(World Tribune Press, Paperback: mail order #4120; $15.00)